Eating, Drinking,
and Visiting in the South

Eating, Drinking, and Visiting in the South

AN INFORMAL HISTORY

Joe Gray Taylor

Illustrations by Charles Shaw

Louisiana State University Press
Baton Rouge and London

Designer: Joanna Hill
Typeface: Primer
Typesetter: G & S Typesetters
Printer: Thomson-Shore
Binder: John Dekker and Sons

Library of Congress Cataloging in Publication Data

Taylor, Joe Gray.
Eating, drinking, and visiting in the South.

Bibliography: p.
Includes index.
1. Food habits—Southern States—History.
2. Drinking customs—Southern States—History.
3. Dinners and dining—Southern States—History.
4. Southern States—Social life and customs—
History.   I. Title.
GT2853.U5T39   394.1'2'0975   81–19326
ISBN 0–8071–0895–2   AACR2
ISBN 0–8071–1013–2 (pbk.)

Louisiana Paperback Edition, 1982
91 90 89   5 4 3 2

Contents

Preface and Acknowledgments / ix

1 Stewpot and Roasting Ears: The Food of the Southern Frontier / 3

2 Pork, Possum, and Even Oysters: Plain Eating in the Old South / 17

3 Corn, Cowpeas, and Company: Plain Eating in the Old South, Continued / 37

4 High on the Hog: Eating on the Great Plantation / 53

5 Grease, Bedbugs, and Good Food: Eating Away from Home in the Old South / 67

6 Cornmeal and Salt Pork: The Food of the Slaves / 83

7 Long Years and Short Rations: The Civil War / 93

8 Bacon, Biscuits, and Sometimes Ham: The New South / 107

9 Eating, Drinking, and Socializing: The New South, Continued / 125

10 Fatback, Pellagra, and Clay Eaters: The Impoverished South / 137

11 The Winds of Change: The Contemporary South / 149

Notes / 159

Bibliographical Essay / 173

Index / 179

TO CHICK AND CLARENCE
Who Provide the Best of Food, Drink, Hospitality
and Friendship

Preface and Acknowledgments

This book had its beginning many years ago in a nostalgic personal essay, "The Food of the New South" (*Georgia Review*, XX [Spring, 1966]), in which I told of the eating during my youth. The essay brought me a probably undeserved reputation as an expert on southern food, and that led to this effort at a survey of southern food, drink, and hospitality as they have developed over the years. No claim to definitiveness is made; not all the regional variations that I know about are described, and undoubtedly there are many others of which I am ignorant. Any attempt at a definitive work on the subject would of necessity be many times the length of this one. I hope that I provide a good description of the subject; little effort has been made at analysis. Finally, I cheerfully confess to having used my own experiences. I have been eating in the South for sixty years, which is a goodly proportion of the time covered.

Most of the works consulted have been diaries, memoirs, family letters, travel accounts, and secondary studies. All have been published. Special recognition must be extended to Sam Bowers Hilliard, whose *Hog Meat and Hoecake: Food Supply in the Old South* (Carbondale: Southern Illinois University Press, 1972) is not only cited frequently in earlier chapters but also was used as a bibliographical guide to many other sources. I owe a personal debt to R.A. Suarez, now retired from McNeese State University, who read the manuscript not once, but twice, and who made critical and helpful suggestions each time. Helen Friday Taylor, my wife, prevented my making some foolish errors and kept me inspired with good southern cooking.

It is necessary also to acknowledge the contributions to this work of my mother, grandmothers, and a host of aunts, cousins, and neighbors in a rural southern community of about a half-century ago. These women formed my tastes in food just as they and their husbands, for good or ill, formed my character. I realize full well that I grew up in an environment that in many respects was far from perfect, but I take tremendous pride in my background and would not change it if I had a chance to do so.

I take full responsibility for any errors of fact or interpretation.

Eating, Drinking, and Visiting in the South

1

Stewpot and Roasting Ears

THE FOOD OF THE SOUTHERN FRONTIER

It is almost an axiom among historians of the American South that much of that region was still frontier at the outbreak of the Civil War. This work does not challenge that assumption, but it does assert that the diet of southerners on what Frederick Jackson Turner called "the cutting edge" of the frontier differed significantly from the diet that came into being after a measure of stability had been achieved. I also agree with Thomas Perkins Abernethy that Saint Augustine, Jamestown, and the first settlements in Maryland and the Carolinas were a European frontier, extensions of Europe across the Atlantic, and that a uniquely American frontier did not come into being until pioneers had pushed into the Piedmont and beyond it.[1]

Settlers along the Atlantic Ocean hugged the coasts and estuaries because they lacked the skills and knowledge needed to attack the great inland wilderness. Their first great adjustment, made most unwillingly, was to learn to eat the foods the Indians ate. It would be difficult to exaggerate the contribution of the American Indian to the diet of the South. Domestic animals played a very small role in southern frontier eating. Most meat continued to be wild, and the methods of hunting and preparing it were in large part learned from the Indians. Fortunately, it should be added, the early settlers rejected the Indian custom of cooking small game by throwing it into the coals, hide, hair, guts, and all.

It was from the Indians that the first settlers learned which wild plant foods were available and how to prepare them. Most important, of course, the Indians taught the first settlers how to grow, prepare, and eat corn. No doubt the English settlers would have preferred wheat bread, or even the rye bread that had been their everyday fare in Britain, but these grains did not thrive in the virgin soils of the New World. Nor did the Indian contribution end with corn. The Irish potato did not come to the South until late, but it was an Indian vegetable. So was the sweet potato, which came early and played a most important role. The Indians gave the South squash, most of the beans that Americans eat until this day, pumpkins, all peppers except black pepper, and probably cowpeas. Tomatoes and eggplants were developed by the Indians, but many southerners looked on them as poisonous until the twentieth century. Even the humble peanut originated in Brazil, but it went to Africa and then came back to Virginia on a slave ship; it was often called by its African name, "goober."

To say that the eighteenth-century pioneer ate much like an Indian and lived to a great extent by eating game is not to say that the first settlers did not do likewise. The first Englishmen in America, those who came to the Atlantic coast and gradually pushed inland, harvested shellfish and caught and ate finned fish. They also hunted and shot game. But as settlement pushed beyond the tidal rivers along the coast, fish became much harder to obtain. On the other hand, the firearms of the eighteenth century were far better than those of the seventeenth, and thus the people who pushed through the mountains were much better equipped to kill an adequate supply of game. In fact, the Tidewater influence on the men and women who settled the western Piedmont and the Great Valley, and who made their way through the mountains, must not be overestimated. Usually, instead of coming westward from the Tidewater, they came down the Great Valley from western Pennsylvania. These later pioneers, indeed, were even different in blood from the earlier settlers. Those who came into the Tidewater were largely English; those who settled the valley and beyond were more often than not Scotch-Irish or German.[2]

These Ulstermen and Germans who led the way into the Old Southwest were accustomed to short rations. Germany had not fully recovered from the devastation of the Thirty Years' War before it was stripped bare again during the wars of Louis XIV. Rhineland peasants were accustomed to danger, hardship, and hunger. In Scotland peasants lived in one-room stone and turf huts with earthen floors, and they cooked and sought warmth at an open fire that was vented through a hole in the roof. In winter they shared the hut with any animals they were fortunate enough to own. In northern Ireland the dwellings were no better, and Ulstermen lived in constant danger from the native Irish who had taken refuge in unsettled areas. Wolves constantly threatened their animals; English economic measures kept them on the verge of starvation. For these people life on the frontier, harsh though it was, was probably an improvement over what they had known. Obviously some people of English stock participated in this stage of the southern frontier, but more often they let the Scotch-Irish and the Germans begin the clearing of the forest, fight the early decisive battles with the Indians, and make an area reasonably safe. Then they went west, armed with money instead of long rifles, and bought the land and the improvements made upon it by the true pioneers.[3]

These first settlers on a frontier had no choice but to depend upon game for sustenance, at least until they could clear a patch of ground and plant corn and vegetables. They much preferred buffalo to other meat, so long as it could be had; buffalo were never overly abundant east of the Mississippi. The hump and the tongue were favorite cuts, but almost the entire animal except offal (the Indians ate the intestines) was devoured. Even after the meat was gone, the pioneer heated the leg bones in the coals of his fire, cracked them open with an axe, and relished the marrow. William Byrd said that the meat of the buffalo was exactly like beef, except that the fat was yellow. But these great animals could not long survive the presence of frontiersmen with long rifles. As early as 1791 a traveler reported that "the Buffaloes have entirely quitted the cultivated parts of Kentucky."[4]

The black bear had an important part in the frontier economy. Until hogs could be established, bear fat was almost the only shortening available for cooking; it also might fuel a smoky, evil-smelling lamp, serve in a pinch as a lubricant, or provide dressing for a swain's hair before he went courting. Bear fat might be stored in a block of wood hollowed out into a sort of barrel, or it might be hung from a peg in a deerskin bag. The bear's tanned hide might serve as a warm wrap in cold weather, as a bed cover, or as a rug. Hungry people would kill a bear any time they could, but in the spring the beasts were poor and strong to the taste; in the fall they were fat and at their best.[5]

Frontier people liked bear meat. If they had salt, they could cure it like pork; bear hams were frequently salted and then smoked. Other cuts might be roasted on a spit or sliced into steaks. A South Carolina cook's recipe for bear steak says that it should be one inch thick and fried until well done. This last was important, said the author, because "otherwise the flavor may be too strong and gamey for the average taste." William Byrd found that bear meat had "a good relish, very savory and inclining nearest to that of pork."[6] Harriette Arnow tells of a "Granma Bull" who set up a sort of open air restaurant on the road into Kentucky during the great migration to that frontier. She had only bear meat and corn bread, and her customers roasted the meat while she made bread; they paid her whatever she asked. The paw of a bear looked remarkably like a human foot, but roasted in the coals it was a frontier favorite. It should not be supposed, however, that every man panted after bear meat. A Methodist circuit rider had announced that he would eat no coon or 'possum, so one family he visited proudly made ready to feed him a fat, newly killed bear. After one look at the carcass, he declined, saying that the bear had "the very foot of a Negro and the tusks of a dog."[7]

Black bears, unlike the buffalo, managed to survive east of the Mississippi and do to this day; but incessant hunting and cutting away the forests soon made them scarce, and hog lard soon replaced bear grease. Venison, however, was probably from the beginning a more important food than bear. The forests of the primitive South abounded in white-tailed deer. Deer hides provided clothing and containers; their antlers were often the racks on which guns or garments rested; and their meat was eaten fresh and preserved. Pioneers roasted venison on a spit over a fire, but if a pot was available, they more than likely made it the main part of a stew. Not only venison went into the pot, but also almost anything else edible the family might have, meat or vegetable. Like bear, deer were fattest in the fall, but a family in need of meat took what it could get regardless of the season. Frontier hunters were not interested in trophies. They much preferred a dry doe or a yearling to a tough old buck with impressive antlers.[8]

Frontiersmen preserved venison by cutting it into strips, then drying and smoking it. This jerky, according to one who had eaten it, was of the consistency of a stick of wood, but it would keep almost indefinitely. In a pinch it could be chewed as it was, but cooks improved it by soaking it in water overnight; then it became the main item in a savory stew. A frontier traveler might carry a "wallet" filled with jerky for himself, just as he carried a sack of shelled corn for his horse. Venison continued to be a much-liked meat long after the early frontier had passed, but never afterward was it such a basic necessity for the preservation of health and strength.[9]

Wild turkey was another mainstay of the frontier diet. These magnificent, unbelievably wary birds, today carefully stocked by state game departments, seem to have been almost as common as blackbirds on the southern frontier. In northern Louisiana, according to one account, they were so abundant that horsemen ran them down and lassoed them! Perhaps this was a tall tale, but it is undeniably a fact that the birds were so numerous that people used the white meat of the breast as bread when eating other viands. When frontiersmen killed large numbers of these great birds, they cut them in half, salted them, and then dried them. Thus preserved they could be brought out later and either put into a stew or fried in bear grease. The stew was more common; William Byrd found a combination of turkey and venison to be "the best soup in the world" when a little rice or barley was added.[10] Fortunately, wild turkeys continued to be available in many parts of the South until after the Civil War. When they disappeared, or

became scarce, domestic turkeys, which through their generations had traveled from Mexico to Europe and Asia and then back
to the New World, replaced them.

Southern frontiersmen ate almost, if not quite, any animal available to them. Opossum and raccoon were favorites from the beginning, the possum taking first place because, like a fall bear, he
abounded in fat. The pioneer also ate squirrel with gusto; one gets
the impression that squirrels were the most plentiful meat in the
stewpot, which almost constantly hung over the coals of the frontier fireplace. The killing and eating of squirrels and coons served
a double purpose, because both animals were fond of corn, and it
was well to reduce their numbers in the vicinity of newly cleared
fields.

The pioneer ate rabbit, of course, and also quail, passenger
pigeons, robins, and almost any other bird. In the autumn, migrating waterfowl might provide many meals, though a fat young buck
or bear seems to have been preferred. The early American devoured with relish some animals not now regarded as edible. William Byrd, among others, thought that bobcat and panther made
fine meat, white like veal and of excellent taste. Beaver tails were
said to make a fine soup except in the summer, when they were
too musky. The situation was perhaps unusual, but a navy-marine
expedition into the Everglades in 1842 ate almost everything in
sight except snakes: alligators, wild hogs, turtles, fish, curlews,
woodpeckers, and even cormorants. The men particularly enjoyed
crane eggs.[11]

Records tell of a great feast on Christmas day, 1778, on the Kentucky side of the Ohio River on the tract that would become Louisville. Among the meats were venison and bear, wild turkey, rabbit,
coon, and even buffalo, accompanied by three kinds of corn bread,
milk, butter, and even homemade cheese. The main attraction,
however, was a very large possum, baked whole, and hanging by
its tail from a piece of wood in the center of the table. While it
lasted, the marsupial was the preferred meat of the feasters. [12]

Away from the coast, southern frontiersmen were usually not
great eaters of fish. Fishing with hook and line normally was not

so productive as hunting, and hooks and nets were scarce and expensive. In many areas fish traps made of pliant wood were set in lakes and streams. Presumably all the fish native to southern rivers and lakes were from time to time caught and devoured, but the catfish, because of its size, relative freedom from bones, and good taste, seems to have been the favorite wherever saltwater fish were not to be had. Thus a lasting southern tradition was born. No doubt frontiersmen sometimes baked fish in clay, and certainly now and then they boiled them, but most of the time fish were fried in whatever kind of fat was available.

The wilderness afforded foods other than animals, birds, and fish. Where it could be found, a weed called "poke" or "poke sallat" ("Cherokee sallat" in East Tennessee), one of the first green things to appear in the spring, was harvested and boiled. In late spring or early summer came wild plums and berries, though these did not thrive except where the virgin forest had been cleared or burned away to afford the bushes some sunlight. In the fall came persimmons, astringent wild grapes, and delicious muscadines. Also ripening in the fall and early winter were nuts, hickory, chinquapin, and the now extinct American chestnut. In times of scarcity nuts were an important part of the frontier diet; if necessary a housekeeper could imitate the Indians and make a clear oil from hickory nuts, though it took many nuts and much labor for a little oil. Also, hickory nuts, cracked fine and added to a stew, made a thickener and seasoning called "sof-ky" by the Indians, "Tom Fuller" by the settlers.[13]

The ambition of the pioneer was to cease being a frontiersman and to become a settled farmer as soon as possible. Often more substantial settlers brought a cow with them. Her breeding might not be very good, and the diet she found in the forest would not improve her scrawny frame, but the scanty milk she provided in the months after calving was literally the difference between life and death for many a frontier child. When the settlers arrived in many parts of the lower South, from Florida to Texas, wild cattle ranged, descended from Spanish stock or herds once owned by Indians. The so-called cattle frontier did not begin in the trans-

Mississippi West after the Civil War; it preceded the agricultural frontier in many parts of the Old South, with roundups, branding, cattle drives, and the other activities associated with cattle grazing. Pioneer southerners were not, however, great eaters of beef; they preferred game or, especially, pork.[14]

Wild hogs found an almost ideal environment in the unsettled South. Roots, young plants, grass, and berries provided forage for them in the spring and summer, and they could fatten on acorns during the fall and winter. The young might fall victim to predators, but mature wild razorback hogs were generally well able to take care of themselves. Anything they could not outfight, they could outrun. To what extent, if any, frontier settlers redomesticated these feral beasts is impossible to say, but the herds they did eventually establish were from the beginning appreciably higher in quality than the wild stock. These domestic swine also ranged the woods freely, fattened primarily on acorns, and had to be hunted down for market or slaughter. As game grew scarce, pork became the primary meat for the South, a position it would hold into the middle of the twentieth century.

Sheep did not thrive on the frontier; they were too easily killed by bears, wolves, and cougars, and the lambs even by bobcats. Those who kept sheep did so primarily for their wool, not for meat. Tidewater Virginians seem to have liked mutton, but the people of the frontier lost their taste for it, if indeed they had ever had it. Most southerners, including me, do not care for mutton to this day. Pioneers did love to eat chickens and eggs, but poultry, too, fell easy victim to almost any predator, including weasels, minks, foxes, coons, possums, snakes, hawks, and owls. By the time a man could depend on chickens and eggs, he no longer lived on the frontier.

Next to keeping his family alive and protecting it from the elements, the most important task of the southern pioneer was clearing land for planting. This was not quickly done; it took one man years of backbreaking labor to clear completely only a few acres of virgin forest, and thus some communal effort was essential. Even if trees were girdled, they eventually had to be burned down or otherwise removed. Cabin raisings and log rollings were important social occasions that persisted long after the frontier had come to an end everywhere, even into the twentieth century; but on the frontier they were essential to survival. If the pioneer got his first patch of land cleared in late summer or early fall, he often planted turnips first, even though corn was the most important crop. The family would have greens a few weeks after planting; the turnips themselves were not the most nourishing of vegetables, but they were filling and provided needed vitamins.[15]

But corn was the staff of life on the southern frontier; most southerners depended upon corn as a major part, if not the most important part, of their nourishment until World War II. It has been suggested that if the American pioneer had had to eat wheat instead of corn it would have taken another hundred years for settlement to reach the Rocky Mountains. "Corn will produce four times as much as wheat per acre and requires only one-tenth the seed . . . . and only one-third the time from planting until it can be used as food." Wheat planted in autumn cannot be harvested for nine months, "whereas a woman can take a . . . . [hoe] in April and with a quart of seed plant a patch around a cabin and in six weeks she and her children can begin to eat roasting ears; and when it gets too hard for that she can parch it."[16]

The woman above would have needed very little equipment to do better than simply parch her corn. With a simple mortar and pestle she could pound it into a coarse meal from which she could make unleavened hoe cake or ash cake to bake on the hoe blade or a board before the fireplace. If she preferred, she could boil the meal in water and make corn meal mush. If she had an ash hopper and leached out lye, she could soak the dry grains and make "big hominy." Then she could dry the big hominy and pound it into "hominy grits," a favorite southern dish to this day. Ordinarily years passed after people came to the frontier before they ate breadstuffs made from any grain other than corn.[17]

Vegetables were important to the frontiersman, and the migrating family often brought seed from the East. Probably sweet potatoes ranked next to turnips in importance, but other vegetables were planted as soon as possible, including peas, pumpkins, beans, and squash. These vegetables were important as individual items of food, but they probably were more important for adding body and flavor to the contents of the stewpot hanging over the fire. The gourd was also an important plant, not so much for food as for making dippers, ladles, and other containers. It should be emphasized, however, that the settler on the cutting edge of the frontier usually had very little land planted in vegetables. By the time he got around to putting in a garden, he was no longer on the frontier.[18]

The most common drink was water, and it came from a stream or a spring. The pioneer digging a well might have died of thirst before he found water. Milk was drunk when it was available. Probably some wine was made from blackberries, and, following Indian example, many pioneers made a sort of beer from persimmons in the fall. But when the pioneer did not drink water, he normally wanted something with a high alcoholic content. On the Atlantic frontier hard cider, rum from New England or the West Indies, or brandy distilled from the abundant "Indian" peaches had served this need for a century. One of the most notable contributions of the Scotch-Irish to American culture, however, was the invention of corn whiskey.[19]

The frontier distiller ground his grain, being careful that it was not too fine or too coarse. He preferred yellow corn if he could get it. This he mixed thoroughly with water in a barrel, two bushels of the grain to fifty gallons of water. Sometimes he added yeast or malt to hasten fermentation, but usually the natural process was sufficient. When fully ready, this mash was run through a still, almost always twice, and each barrel would produce about five gallons of 110-proof whiskey. An experienced distiller could make a fair estimate of proof by shaking the liquid in a glass container and then observing the "bead" as it subsided, but a better test was to drop a pinch of tallow into the liquor. If it sank to the bottom quickly, the whiskey was too strong and water was added. If the tallow floated, it was probably necessary to run the whiskey through the still again. Ideally, the tallow sank to the bottom slowly but steadily.

Frontiersmen drank tremendous quantities of whiskey. It was the accepted tranquilizer, stimulant, disinfectant, and anesthetic. Babies took a weak toddy to satisfy them with their new environment; the mother took a stronger toddy to reward her for her labor; and the father drank whiskey straight to help him bear up under the strain. It is obvious that the pioneer liked the taste of whiskey; he made no attempt to disguise it. He drank it at the table like tea or coffee, and when a guest came to his house, be it neighbor, relative, statesman, or clergyman, he would have been humiliated if he had not been able to offer him a drink.[20]

Historians debate how widespread drunkenness was on the frontier. Common sense suggests that people on the edge of settlement were careful to keep their wits about them as long as Indians threatened, but probably there was some loosening of self-control once it was safe to get drunk. An Anglican priest, certainly not unbiased, preached to a group of Scotch-Irish Presbyterian frontiersmen in western South Carolina shortly before the American Revolution. He said they had never heard a sermon or the Lord's Prayer. After the service, according to his account, "they went out to revelling, Drinking, Singing, Dancing, and Whoring, and most of the Company were drunk before I quitted the spot."[21]

Much has been written about frontier hospitality, and from secondary sources one could form a picture of a society that with open heart and hands welcomed all who came. One historian asserts that on the frontier "even poverty was no excuse for lack of hospitality as many a visitor found when he knocked at the door of a miserable cabin on the fringes of settlement . . . . All that the owner possessed was freely given, and offers to pay indignantly refused." Another avers that "hospitality was the rule on the fringe of settlement. People were isolated, lonely, hungry for companionship and news."[22] Certainly frontier people were hungry for news, and many travelers reported on their insatiable curiosity, which embraced every imaginable bit of knowledge about the traveler. But the evidence concerning hospitality is curiously conflicting. The Dukes of Orleans ate bear meat and corn bread frequently on their western travels, but the families with whom they stayed expected to be paid. John Sevier, one of the most admired men of the Old Southwest, always paid for his meals except when visiting old friends, and even the revered Bishop Francis Asbury almost always paid for his board and lodging. On the other hand, William Bartram and John Bradbury seem to have been welcomed gladly and freely wherever they went.[23]

Even on the frontier, a traveler was wise to have letters of introduction. If these were not available but one rode a good horse, wore good clothes, and had the speech of a gentleman, he might very well be hospitably received by equals and inferiors. But if the traveler was poorly dressed, badly mounted, and ill spoken, his reception was likely at best to be grudging. Probably he was fortunate if, instead of being lodged for vagrancy in the new-built jail, he was given a firm admonition to get out of the settlement. It could hardly have been otherwise. The leading men on the frontier were more often than not related to leading families in the longer-settled regions; and whatever the leveling effect of the frontier on the future, when it existed it was still an aristocratic society. Also there was the simple matter of safety. The frontiers east of the Mississippi were infested by outlaws who could have frightened Billy the Kid into hysteria. The saddle-weary, unshaven, unkempt man who knocked on the settler's door at nightfall might be one of the murderous Harpe brothers or perhaps one of John Murrel's bloodthirsty clan, and only a fool would have welcomed him.

2

Pork, Possum, and Even Oysters
PLAIN EATING IN THE OLD SOUTH

Any distinction between antebellum southern life on the frontier and that life after the frontier had ceased to be is necessarily
arbitrary. In Texas a real Indian-fighting frontier persisted after
the Civil War, and in hundreds of areas west of the Appalachians,
and in the Appalachians, where no navigable stream ran and where
no railroad penetrated, frontierlike conditions persisted well after
Appomattox. This was especially true in the so-called piney-woods
sections where stock grazing was the chief means of livelihood. In
the 1840s, for example, families living in the pine woods of southern
Mississippi and Alabama had "abundance and variety of food," including "turkey, venison, bear meat, fish, and other wild game
from woods and stream." They also had quantities of pork, beef,
dairy products, and a few vegetables, especially sweet potatoes,
which they probably would not have had on a new frontier in the
process of settlement. Well into the twentieth century, people in
the "Big Thicket" of east Texas lived lives that corresponded closely
to those of men and women on the eighteenth-century frontier.[1]

Doubtless many of the dishes served on the frontier tables were
savory and appetizing, but doubtless also many of them were
pretty bad. The pioneer who ate panther, beaver-tail soup, boar-
bear meat, and the flesh of bucks shot during the rut could not
afford taste buds that were too discriminating. The southern frontiersman took more pride in having enough and more food for his
family and guests than he did in the gustatory quality of that food.
The antebellum southerner thus inherited from his frontier back-

ground more respect for "big eating" than for fine eating. Obviously every normal host and hostess wanted their food to be good, but like the English yeomen of Elizabeth's time, they were more concerned with quantity and variety than with quality in the gourmet sense. Some of the dishes of the Old South were as good as any in the world, however, and this should not be forgotten.[2]

Southerners of different social and economic levels took their meals at different times. The family of a wealthy planter might delay breakfast until half past nine in the morning, but the farmer who worked his own fields, the townsman who opened his own shop, and even the planter who served as his own overseer took this first meal of the day at or soon after sunrise. Whenever they ate, they ate heartily. European travelers, accustomed even then to the relatively sparse continental breakfast, were amazed at the quantities downed by Americans.[3] Dinner, the main meal of the day, might come at noon, but it was most often served after one o'clock in the afternoon and sometimes after three o'clock. Supper, the evening meal, was ordinarily made up of leftovers and served cold, except that sometimes hot bread was prepared. Mrs. Charles Colcock Jones, mistress of several plantations, noted in a letter that because she had expected a special guest, "We had a *hot* supper."[4]

Almost all cooking was done in a fireplace. In a family's original log cabin, and many prospering families remained in a log cabin for a generation or more, the fireplace was in the room where other indoor activities went on. If a larger home was built, the kitchen, with a fireplace designed more for cooking than for heating, was usually separate from the house. This kept cooking odors from the living quarters, and the danger of fire was lessened. A few wood-burning stoves came into use, especially in the towns, before the Civil War, but such modernity came to most homes after the war—sometimes long after.

The kitchen fireplace could be supplied with elaborate utensils. On a built-in ledge lay the backbar, sometimes as much as six feet from the fireplace floor. Hooks of various lengths hung from the backbar, designed so that pots and kettles could hang at various distances from the fire. Trivets of various heights sat on the floor so that food could be placed at exactly the desired distance from the coals. Usually an elaborate fireplace such as this would include a spit for roasting large pieces of meat. Such a kitchen would also afford iron and brass skillets—not frying pans, but baking utensils with legs and lids so that coals could be raked overhead and beneath—frying pans, special long-handled forks, ladles, waffle irons, chafing dishes, and saucepans. The kitchen of a Virginia estate inventoried in 1780 contained a thirty-two pound brass kettle, four iron pots ranging from thirty-three to fifty pounds, three skillets, three spits, a frying pan, a mortar and pestle, and a "flesh fork." Often inventories showed scales and various liquid measures (a noggin was equivalent to a pint). At the other extreme, a poor family might possess only a pot, or a pot and a frying pan, with perhaps some kind of a kettle for heating water.[5]

A few of the great plantations boasted silverware and fine china dishes, but even the simplest earthenware dishes were not common in the homes of ordinary people until well into the nineteenth century. On the frontier and for decades after it passed, people most commonly ate from wooden dishes. Often spoons were the only tool, and each member of the family dipped each bite directly from the cooking pot. As time passed, wooden trenchers were carved, and finally a wooden bowl for each member of the family. In time pewter spoons, bowls, forks, and plates replaced wood, though many families still preferred to use wooden bowls and platters in the kitchen. Eventually the pewter gave way to earthenware, but many men objected to glazed dishes, complaining that their hard surface dulled knives.[6] As the nineteenth century advanced, the industrial revolution made earthenware, and even fine china, cheaper and much easier to obtain.

Many women kept collections of recipes and passed them on to their daughters, and there was much trading of recipes among friends. A few cookbooks were available. The earlier ones came from England, but *Mrs. Randolph's Cookery Book* was famous in the early nineteenth century. It was reported, though not confirmed, that the author of this work had spent three fortunes developing her dishes. Even so, such recipes were for upper-class homes; far too many people of the lower or middle class did not read well enough to make use of published recipes. They learned to cook, usually, from their mothers, and any experiments they might make were more likely to result from necessity than from any attempt to improve the fare they put on their tables. Even the highly literate plantation mistress must have had troubles cooking by recipe; she did not do her own cooking but depended on slave women who might or might not understand and follow directions.[7]

One must remember that cooking in some parts of the South varied greatly from that in other parts. If travelers can be believed, the more recently an area had been settled, the worse the food was likely to be. But there were significant differences in culinary customs, too. A family in the Piedmont might find the seafoods of coastal Carolina or the Chesapeake Bay region unappetizing. Some who did not hunt never learned to appreciate the gamey taste of venison or waterfowl. An Anglican missionary found the food of backwoodsmen in South Carolina "exceedingly filthy and most execrable," made up almost entirely of "clabber, butter, fat musty bacon, and cornbread." Louisiana's Creole cooking did not appeal to all. One unhappy sojourner wrote that "In no country that ever I have seen is so little attention paid to comfortable living as among the common people of Louisiana and Mississippi." Even less-prejudiced observers looked askance at the drinking of *café au lait* by children and had deep private thoughts about what might be the ingredients of the gumbo that was set before them in Creole homes.[8]

The corn bread that most southerners ate daily had some definite disadvantages, chief of these the fact that it did not keep well; even so, in most cases it seems to have been preferred even when other breads might have been had. The southern love of corn bread may be easier to understand if one remembers that the peasants of Europe usually ate rye bread, or even oatcakes, rather than wheaten bread. Incidentially, of necessity the Creoles of Louisiana ate corn bread, but they did not like it. Southern corn bread improved with time. Using better cooking utensils and adding milk, eggs, and perhaps even a little wheat flour to the batter, a cook could produce a variety rather than simple unleavened pones baked before the fire.[9]

Practical reasons as well as taste preference explain the southern fondness for corn bread. When annual rainfall nears fifty inches, as it does in much of the South, wheat is subject to rust. This fungus does not prohibit the growing of wheat, but it does reduce the yield. Corn demanded little skill in cultivation, and it was certainly easier to gather a given amount of corn than to harvest half as much wheat. Probably most important of all, corn was much easier to process with the crude machinery available. Slow-moving and ill-matched millstones that could grind corn into an acceptable meal only stirred wheat into a glutinous mess. Too, the choice was not between corn bread and the flour biscuit that southerners came to love in later years. Commercial baking powder did not become available until a few years before the Civil War, and homemade baking powder was difficult to make and unreliable. No one had yet dreamed of self-rising flour.[10]

If a family ate wheat bread, almost always it was yeast bread. Yeast bread made from home-ground flour must have been good, but also it took much more preparation than corn bread. A major inconvenience was that it had to be made up the night before cooking so that the dough could rise before it went into the oven. As might be expected, the amount of wheaten bread consumed rose with wealth and social position; however, more of it was consumed in the border states than in the Deep South. Also, wheat bread was more popular in the towns where there were commercial bakers. It was not unknown for planters to take loaves of white bread home with them when they returned from town.[11]

As game became scarce, southerners depended more and more on pork as their chief meat, something about which they did not complain. The large amount of pork consumed, and the frequency with which it appeared on the table, was noted by foreign travelers, by northerners who had come South, and by southerners themselves, inevitably with disapproval. William Byrd noted that pork was "the staple commodity of North Carolina and . . . with pitch and tar makes up the whole of their traffic . . . . These people live so much upon swine's flesh that it don't [sic] only incline them to the yaws, and consequently to the . . . [loss] of their noses, but makes them likewise extremely hoggish in their temper, and many of them seem to grunt rather than speak in their ordinary conservation."[12] Dr. John S. Wilson, a resident of Columbus, Georgia, opposed so much pork eating and opined that the United States might "properly be called the great Hog-eating Confederacy or the Republic of Porkdom." At any rate, should the South and West "be named dietetically, the above appellation would be peculiarly appropriate; for in many parts of this region, so far as meat is concerned, it is fat bacon and pork, fat bacon and pork only, and that continually morning, noon, and night, for all classes, sexes, ages, and conditions; and except for the boiled bacon and collards at dinner, the meat is generally fried, and thus supersaturated with grease in the form of hog's lard." In making fun of the southerner's fondness for pork, however, one must bear in mind that even unusually poor southerners of the antebellum period, as a French traveler noted, were "better fed and clad here than in any other country."[13]

There were good reasons why southerners ate so much pork. A pig born in the spring was ready for slaughter in early winter, obviating the necessity for carrying anything other than breeding stock over the winter. Swine largely supported themselves in the woods during the spring, summer,.and fall. They made efficient use of sweet potato vines, orchard fruit that fell to the ground, and unharvested small grain or peas. They could be penned and fattened on corn for a few weeks before killing, but this was not always done; many southern farmers went into the woods for their winter meat and took it as it came. Compared to other animals, hogs were efficient in converting grain to meat. One estimate is that 24 percent of the energy of grain eaten by hogs is made available for human consumption as compared to 18 percent for milk products and only 3½ percent for beef and mutton.[14]

The ordinary southern hog was no beast of beauty, and he hardly seemed the same species as the show hog of today's county fair. He was long, lean, thin, large-headed, high in the shoulder, and low at the rump, built for speed and self-defense rather than meat. One Englishman wrote that "the real American hog is what is termed the wood hog; they are long in the leg, narrow in the back, short in the body, flat in the sides with a long snout, very rough in their hair. . . . They will go to a distance from a fence, take a run, and leap through the rails three or four feet from the ground, turning themselves sidewise."[15]

Razorbacks answering the above description, except possibly for the "sidewise" leap through a rail fence, are still to be found in parts of the South today, but by the 1840s a good beginning had been made at improving the breed. Progressive agriculturists imported well-bred boars from England and the North, and the male descendants of these animals found their way to smaller farms and plantations. Young boars that would not be needed for breeding were castrated and eventually slaughtered. During these years so many wild razorback boars were about that gilts not wanted as brood sows were spayed before being turned loose in the woods. Sows kept for breeding obviously had to be kept safe from undesirable interlopers.[16]

A suckling pig (*cochon au lait* in Louisiana) or one a few weeks past weaning might be cooked almost any time of year. "Mother sends . . . her special thanks for the pig, which was roasted on Saturday," one lady wrote to another in the spring of 1855. A larger animal might be barbecued at any season, the Fourth of July being especially favored for this treat.[17] Even so, the first spell of freezing weather that looked as though it would last for several days was the time when most hogs were killed. If there were many animals to be slaughtered, other hog-killing days would come later, but the first one was the most important. It made fresh meat available to people who were famished for it, and it gave promise of meat through the long winter to come.

Southerners slaughtered their hogs as early in the morning as possible, as soon as there was good light, and then dipped the carcasses in inclined barrels filled with scalding water from a boiling pot or heated by dropping hot stones into them. The hot water loosened the pig's bristles which then could be scraped from the skin with a knife or even a spoon. When well scraped, the porkers were suspended by the hind legs from a frame erected for the purpose or from a handy tree limb. A pole behind the Achilles' tendon held the legs apart. Then the belly was slit open and the interior organs removed. The liver was prized and often eaten the night after the hogs were killed. The brains might grace the breakfast table the next morning, mixed with eggs if the poultry had been productive. The chitterlings, or small intestines, were carefully cleaned and then cooked in batter to the delight of white and black alike. The backbone, tenderloin, tongue, ears, and tail also were eaten soon after the hog was killed. The feet and especially the "knuckles" (ankles) were special delicacies.

The jowls were removed from the head and cured like bacon. When New Year's Day came, hog jowls and field peas, or hog jowls and greens, depending upon the part of the South, were eaten to bring good luck as well as to provide a treat. The rest of the head was made into hog's head cheese, more often called souse, a dish popular in England in Elizabethan times. In the early years scraps of lean meat were pounded into sausage; well before the Civil War, hand mills were available for grinding and thus saved hours of labor. Fat, some from the meat that was to be eaten right away, some from parts intended for curing, some the leaf fat, which was from inside the abdomen and was especially thick about the kidneys, was one of the most important products of hog killing. Boiled in an iron pot, it was rendered into lard, which served as grease for frying and shortening for bread. The solids remaining in the pot after the lard had been rendered, called "cracklins," could be eaten as they were, but they were at their best when mixed with corn bread batter and made into cracklin bread. One heretofore unmentioned by-product was the bladder; it was inedible, but it could be blown up and kicked about by children; until the twentieth century it was the nearest thing to a balloon that most southern farm children saw. The lungs or "lights," were seldom eaten in the Old South, and the kidneys almost never.[18]

Hams, shoulders, sides of bacon, and pieces of fatback from between the rib cage and the skin above the true bacon sides were cured for future use. Salt was essential to the curing process, and one of the disadvantages of frontier life was the scarcity of salt. Usually, by the time settlers had hogs enough for curing on a large scale, salt was available either commercially or from a salt lick within reach of the settlement. After the parts to be cured had been trimmed they were liberally covered with salt to draw out blood. Then these parts were buried in salt in a meat box for a month to six weeks. Taken from the box, they were washed and then hung in a smokehouse to be slowly smoked, preferably in smoke from hickory wood. At this stage there were scores of variations; many farmers had more or less secret recipes involving pepper, alum, ashes, molasses, sugar, saltpeter, and other materials that they believed made their cured pork superior. One very sensible practice was rubbing large quantities of red pepper into the exposed joints; otherwise skipper flies laid their eggs on the unprotected area and their larvae bored through the meat. Some planters and farmers, especially those who lived far enough south that there was considerable danger of spoilage when the curing method described above was used, quite literally pickled their pork in barrels of brine. Meat so pickled would not spoil, and awkwardly shaped pieces such as the head could be preserved as easily as hams or shoulders. On the other hand, the meat had to be soaked in water for a long time before cooking or it was simply too salty to eat.[19]

Fresh pork lasted only a short time, sausage a little longer. Cured pork, however, would keep in the smokehouse indefintely, and in the form of ham, shoulder, bacon, or fatback, it appeared on most southern tables every day and at almost every meal until it had all been eaten. In the Deep South, where the weather was warmer and spoilage more likely, cured or pickled pork was often imported from farther north. Cincinnati was famous as "Porkopolis," but Tennessee and Kentucky also prepared much pork for export to the South. In those areas where pork was produced for export, swine or products thereof were almost a medium of exchange. If money was scarce, the value of almost anything could be expressed in live hogs, hams, bacon, or lard.[20]

No great amount of imagination was expended on methods of cooking pork. Liver, sausage, and chops were almost invariably fried. Other pieces of fresh meat were more often boiled, though chitterlings, after being cleaned, soaked in water for more than a day, and then parboiled, were fried before they came to the table. Backbone was often boiled with rice in the Carolina and Georgia low country to produce a *pileau*, usually pronounced "perlu." Hams and shoulders could be baked or boiled, and on plantations they were often so prepared. However, not many ordinary families could afford to set forth a whole, or even a half, ham at one time. In the average household the housewife cut as many slices of ham as the family needed for the next meal and then fried it. Bacon, too, was normally fried when it was served as a meat dish. Much of the bacon, though, went into the pot with vegetables to give them flavor. It was generally regarded as the best thing to come out of the pot and was often reserved for the head of the house. The grease left over from frying pork could itself be used for seasoning vegetables as they boiled, but it was more often poured, hot, over bread. Red-eye gravy, a mixture of pork grease and water, was especially delectable.

The Old South was a major cattle-producing region. The Spaniards first introduced cattle into the savannas of central Florida, and that state has had an important cattle industry ever since. In Texas Spanish cattle had become so numerous by the end of the Civil War that they provided the foundation of the range-cattle industry of the Great Plains. Likewise, the prairies of southwest Louisiana were first stocked with cattle of Spanish ancestry. Because land grants in the southern English colonies were not contiguous but scattered about, leaving much unclaimed land between them, the availability of public grazing land encouraged a cattle frontier in the Piedmont and on across the Appalachians. The "civilized" Indian tribes of the South also kept cattle; many of these ran wild, and others were left behind when their owners were dispossessed

and forced to move to Indian territory. Although southerners preferred pork, beef was available to most of those who might want
it.[21]

Beef was the staple meat in a few parts of the Old South, in
thinly inhabited Florida, in southwest Louisiana, and in Texas. It
would appear, also, that the higher a family's social and economic
status, the more beef it would consume. Southerners as a whole,
however, averaged five pounds of pork to one pound of beef. This
estimate includes slaves, who got an even greater proportion of
pork than did whites; therefore, the average white may have consumed as much as fifty pounds of beef per year, one pound of beef
for two and a half pounds of pork. Even if a lower figure of twenty-
five to thirty pounds of beef per year be accepted, that is still twice
as much beef as the average southerner was reported to be eating
during the 1920s.[22]

Technically, southerners ate more veal than true beef. The average cow or steer, fully grown, weighed from five hundred to seven
hundred pounds and dressed out about half that much. An animal
that had grown to maturity in the woods or on the prairies of Florida, southwestern Louisiana, or Texas was a tough beast in every
way. Steaks had to be beaten, literally, to a pulp before they could
be cooked and brought to the table tender; a roast, after boiling
from dawn to midafternoon, was still as stringy as the canned Australian bully beef that some unfortunate Allied troops, including
me, had to eat during World War II. Because beef was so tough,
southerners preferred to kill and eat younger animals, either calves
or yearlings. To this day southerners eat more veal and less beef
than people in other parts of the nation.[23]

Much beef or veal, like other meat, was fried in pork fat. Steaks
were seldom broiled, but larger cuts often were roasted on a spit
over the coals of a fireplace. Roasts were often boiled, frequently
with vinegar added to the water for flavoring and tenderizing.
Sometimes a whole carcass was barbecued; the farther to the
southwest one traveled, the more common was this practice. Beef
was also pickled in brine and sometimes preserved in dry salt; in
the latter case it was described as "corned beef." Pickled beef, cut

into small bits and dried, became "chipped beef." It would play a large role in feeding twentieth-century soldiers. The internal organs of beef were not as flavored as those of swine, but calf liver was a delicacy, and tripe was a special dish for many. Incidentally, southerners were more likely to eat beef in summer and fall when the supply of cured pork had been exhausted.[24]

Antebellum southerners were not great eaters of mutton. Some planters now and then killed sheep for their families and their slaves, and upper-class town families, especially those who lived in the Atlantic states, ate lamb or mutton fairly often. Probably as many sheep were raised for their flesh as for their wool, but it would also appear that the chief role for many was to serve as animated mowing machines for a planter's lawn. The grazing of sheep continued to pose difficulties; no sooner had the predators that fed upon frontier sheep been checked than they were replaced by packs of wild and domestic dogs that ravaged flocks just as savagely. Most sheep were scrubs, but the quality was gradually being improved by selective breeding. Thomas Dabney of Mississippi used Southdown rams, and on one occasion a saddle of his mutton was so heavy that it tore itself from the spit on which it roasted. Dabney, incidentally, butchered lambs twice a week in spring and summer; the equally aristocratic Charles Colcock Jones family of Georgia ate mutton often and made presents of it to particular friends.[25]

The milch cow was an almost essential possession for a family in the Old South, and more substantial families had several cows so that at least one would be "fresh," that is, giving milk, at any time. Not only country people kept cows; so did most people who lived in little, and sometimes large, towns. Only the more prosperous could afford to buy milk and butter, and one could put more trust in the milk and butter prepared in his own household than in that which came from elsewhere.

The ordinary milch cow of the antebellum South was not a thing of beauty. She was small, lean, and of no certain breed; her milk production would have earned her a quick trip to the slaughterhouse in today's efficient world. Not only did she not give much milk; once her calf was taken from her or weaned, she would "go dry" out of sheer perversity if not "stripped clean" at each milking. As often as not her temper could have borne improvement; the would-be milker who approached her timidly might well be kicked or subjected to some less painful but more humiliating indignity. A few planters imported bred cattle, but most animals ran free in the woods at least from the time the crops were in until time for spring planting. Under such circumstances selective breeding was as impossible as it had been on the medieval common.

The milk, once taken from the cow, was often drunk warm. No refrigeration existed except that nature provided in winter, but fortunate families did have a springhouse located in a shady spot where water from a spring or, perhaps, a running stream cooled the milk and delayed souring. The springhouse not only kept milk, butter, melons, and the like cool in summer; it also prevented freezing in winter. In the early nineteenth century, milk was stored almost entirely in wooden containers; by the time of the Civil War crockery jars were becoming more widely available, but wood was still common. Such containers were not easy to keep clean, but the housewife worked at it. Cleanliness was an absolute necessity in dealing with milk.

Milk not drunk fresh was set aside until the cream rose to the top and the remainder curdled or, as the southerner said, "clabbered." The housewife then poured clabber and cream into a churn, often a beautifully constructed wooden vessel which was sometimes even bound by brass bands. The contents were agitated by a "dasher," which operated through a hole in the center of a tightly fitted hand-carved lid. Making butter was an art. A child could operate the dasher, and frequently did, but when the butter began to form in the churn, only an experienced housekeeper knew when to gather it, when or whether to add water to hasten its coming, how to work it, and how to wash it until all sourness was gone. The child who had done the churning might be allowed to operate the mold which shaped the butter for the table and added a geometric or floral design to the top. Butter varied in color from almost white to yellow gold. One often knew which cow was responsible for a particular pound.

When the butter had been taken away, buttermilk remained in the churn. Cooled in the springhouse, it was delicious to drink and, filled as it was with tiny flecks of butter, had more than a few calories to contribute. Some preferred it fresh; others liked it astringently sour. The only possible objection to it was that it tended to give those who drank too much a rumbling case of "swell bells." It was useful in making corn bread or wheat-flour biscuits; many, indeed, preferred buttermilk bread to that made with whole milk. A southern supper often consisted of a glass or bowl of buttermilk into which corn bread had been crumbled—an almost daily meal for many slave children.

Many poorer southerners never saw butter; all the milk they could obtain they drank whole. Milk from which the cream had been skimmed (skim milk or "blue john") was not wasted, nor was clabber. Clabber, in particular, supplied nourishment for hungry adults and children, and if people were not hungry enough, chickens and hogs would take all the clabber they could get. A few antebellum housewives put curds into cloth bags, squeezed out the whey, let the remaining solids dry on a clothesline, and thus produced cottage cheese. Overall, however, southerners made very little cheese of any kind. Ice cream was known in England before Jamestown, and George Washington had some sort of mechanical device for freezing. Commercial freezers were familiar before the Civil War, and the ice cream man was selling his wares at ten cents the glass in small towns in 1858 or earlier.[26]

A special guest in an antebellum southerner's home could probably anticipate being served chicken. In late spring and through the summer this would probably be fried chicken, always a great favorite with young and old, but in fall or winter an older bird, boiled or roasted, was sacrificed and placed before the guest. Preachers were rumored to have extraordinary appetites for chicken, and an oft-told joke concerned the flock of hens that had learned to disappear into the woods whenever a well-dressed stranger appeared on the place. Chicken was a luxury food, one for special occasions. After the guests had gone, the family might eat leftovers made into a pie with wheat-flour dumplings, but the family eating alone seldom tasted freshly prepared poultry.

Chickens were much more common than any other domestic birds; they were almost self-supporting, feeding themselves fairly well on graze and animal droppings. Furthermore, hens were good mothers and brought up their own progeny with little help from their owners. Chickens and turkeys suffered from predators, but they were protected to some degree because they roosted off the ground. Turkeys, nonetheless, were much harder to raise than chickens. They were especially subject to diseases, and a flock of young birds might be stampeded by a thunderstorm or almost anything else and never be seen again. Obviously, those who did raise turkeys found them a welcome addition to the table, but this was more often the table of a plantation than that of a farm. The farmer would eat wild turkey as long as he could, but he would then fall back on the chicken rather than raise his own turkeys. A very few farmers kept guinea hens, but they were desired more as watchdogs and ornamentals than as food. The idea of a guinea being fine food was snickered at in the South well after the mid-twentieth century.

Some families kept geese and ducks, but they were harder to raise than chickens for the simple reason that they roosted on the ground, where the usual predators approached them easily. Furthermore, ducklings and goslings were easy prey for black bass and snapping turtles, and adult birds made a good lunch for an alligator. Ducks were in general not highly regarded as food, but many people preferred goose to turkey because turkey meat was so dry. A very few antebellum southerners kept pigeons and thus were able to eat squab from time to time. In south Louisiana squab was an especially favored dish in many households.

Many people ate duck eggs, and the eating of guinea eggs was not unknown. Goose and turkey eggs seem to have served only to produce more geese and turkeys. Chicken eggs, of course, were a favorite food, and from early spring through summer, the months when they were widely available, they were eaten in great numbers. Antebellum southerners preferred their eggs, like most other things, fried, but nobody turned up his nose at boiled eggs. Boiled eggs kept for some time and were not uncommon provision for lunch away from home. But hens, living almost in a state of nature, laid few eggs in winter, and the family's egg appetite had to be curbed during the cold months. Most town families also kept chickens, and eggs were important in their diet—as were the birds themselves.[27]

Southerners continued to eat game, though the larger wild animals came to the table less often. Even so, well into the nineteenth century, a prominent lady of Monroe, Louisiana, was reported to have served roasted bear as the main dish at a formal dinner party.[28] Venison remained fairly common, but small game was much more important. Raccoons and possum could still be caught by those who liked to hunt at night, and they continued to be favored dishes. Squirrels remained abundant in most parts of the South throughout the antebellum period; parboiled and fried, cooked with dumplings, or as the base of a stew, they were much appreciated. As fields were cleared and cultivated, cottontail rabbits multiplied mightily, and, prepared in the same ways as squirrels, they probably were the most often eaten game of all. Certainly they were after the Civil War. Coons and possums were roasted, often with sweet potatoes. In Kentucky a soup known as "burgoo" was cooked out of doors, and when available, small game provided the meat. In states farther south a richer mixture known as Brunswick stew was favored; squirrels often provided the meat, but other game, chicken, or pork could be mixed with the vegetables. There were many regional variations.[29]

For those southerners fortunate enough to live along the Atlantic or Gulf coasts, or near the Mississippi or one of its tributaries, waterfowl might be an important part of the diet in fall and winter. This was definitely true on the coasts, but in the interior, references to waterfowl are not so numerous as might have been expected. Perhaps the fact that the best time for waterfowl hunting coincided with the harvest and with the best time for hunting other game accounts for this neglect. Ducks and geese from the wild were either roasted, boiled, or, especially in Louisiana, made into a stew or gumbo. The cooking was simpler than it is today, because the antebellum southerner seems to have had little if any aversion to the gamey taste that modern cooks seek to remove.[30]

Passenger pigeons migrated in countless numbers over much of the South during the first third of the nineteenth century, but long before the Civil War, as the cutting of forests deprived them of the acorns that made up their most important food, they were beginning to decline substantially. Wild turkeys, except in relatively newly settled areas, were no longer abundant. Quail and mourning dove, on the other hand, grew more numerous as the forests were cleared away and grass and weeds provided more feed and, in the case of quail, shelter for them. Both of these small birds were considered delicacies, as they should have been. Snipe, woodcock, and rail were sought by some hunters. Much more commonly eaten, because they were so easy to kill, were robins, which were reported to be delicious in early spring as they fattened on earthworms. Small game was not reserved for hunters' tables; the markets in cities and small towns afforded almost any native game imaginable at remarkably low cost.[31]

Fish and shellfish were an important part of the diet of the coastal South. Shad, mullet, mackerel, croaker, flounder, weakfish, black drum, channel bass, and striped bass were among the varieties caught in the surf, bays, and tidal rivers. Fish from deeper waters, especially grouper and red snapper, seem to have been the prey of commercial fisherman only, but the bay fish were caught by both commercial and sports fishermen. Many plantations had one or more slaves whose primary duty in the summer and fall was to keep the table at the big house supplied with fish. Shrimp, crab, and oysters were all favored shellfish. The first two were almost always boiled, but peeled shrimp and soft-shell crabs were delicious fried. Oysters were, of course, eaten raw, baked in seaweed, fried, and broiled. All along the coasts, shellfish were main items in soups and stews; in Louisiana a seafood gumbo might contain almost anything; it was highly seasoned and thickened with filé, the dried green leaves of the sassafras tree.

In the interior the catfish, which the frontiersmen had favored, continued to be the favorite fish of southerners, as it is to the time of this writing. There were at least four varieties of freshwater catfish, some reaching a weight of more than one hundred pounds. Sports fishermen and netters caught many other kinds of fish, of course. The fish fry was a favorite summer occasion. One traveler noted that the fish fries were held about every two weeks on the Virginia coast during the season; twenty or thirty men gathered to drink whiskey and eat fried fish and soft-shell crabs. Elsewhere on the coast or in the interior the fish fry was more likely to be a group of families enjoying themselves together. Fish spoiled so easily and transportation was so slow that it was more sensible to take the people to the fish than the fish to the people.

After fast steamboats began to ply southern rivers and, especially, after railroads provided even faster transportation, more and more oysters were transported inland. Oyster eating became almost a fad, and those who could afford it always tried to have oysters at Christmas. Getting the bivalves inland in a condition fit for consumption was difficult at best; in those months without an *r* it was almost impossible. But in the fall and winter, places as far from salt water as Memphis and Louisville enjoyed oyster feasts. Sometimes the oysters were packed in ice; sometimes they were kept alive in salt water until delivered to their destination; in very cold weather they were packed only in Spanish moss. Accounts of oyster parties indicate gargantuan consumption.[32]

Less common fish and reptiles were eaten here and there, especially in Louisiana. By diligent use of spices, Creoles and Acadians made normally unattractive fish such as the bowfin and garfish not only edible but good. Common crayfish, found all over the South, were a delicacy only in areas where the French had settled; boiled, stewed, or made into a bisque and served with rice, they pleased. Alligator, though not the best meat in the world, was eaten from time to time. Turtle was enjoyed everywhere, sea turtle being a great favorite along the coasts of South Carolina, Georgia, and Florida. In the interior the soft-shell turtle, the loggerhead, and the vicious snapping turtle were all prized as soup stock. Terrapin soup was favored, of course, on the Chesapeake, but another variety of turtle, also called terrapin by people who spoke English, was almost domesticated in antebellum Louisiana.[33] All over the South, except perhaps in some mountainous areas, people loved to eat the hind legs of the giant bullfrogs that filled the swamps with noise, though there were those who lost their appetites as frog legs continued to kick while they were frying.

3

Corn, Cowpeas, and Company

PLAIN EATING IN THE OLD SOUTH, CONTINUED

Corn was as important as a table vegetable as it was as a bread-stuff. The hominy and hominy grits that had sustained the pioneer continued to grace the tables of his children and grandchildren, and green corn was a food anticipated and enjoyed by almost everyone. Cornmeal mush, nothing more than cornmeal boiled with water and known as "cush-cush" in South Louisiana, was often served at breakfast or supper, especially to children. Usually it was mixed with milk. Hominy and grits also were boiled; often an eater with a keen palate added butter to the grits when it arrived at the table. People might roast green corn in the shuck, whence the name roasting ear, but they also boiled it on the cob, cut it off the cob, and cooked it with water and lard or pork drippings, and even cut the grain off the cob, boiled it, and then fried it into corn fritters.[1]

Turnips, which had been so important a source of greens and therefore of vitamins to the pioneer, continued to be important to the southern farmer until after World War II. Many buried the bottoms in a "hill" of earth and decaying vegetable matter that created enough heat to keep them from freezing. Turnips alone were merely something to eat, cooked or raw. With greens and ham hock or hog jowl they became a delicacy, something to be eagerly anticipated and delightfully remembered.[2]

Sweet potatoes, because they took longer to mature, had not been so important as turnips to the pioneer, but they were exceedingly important to the settled farmer. He put seed potatoes in protected beds in late winter or early spring, and slips came up in the bed. He then transplanted the slips to the fields. By midsummer some potatoes were to be found under the vines, but not nearly so many as would develop later. Most families, and especially children, began digging potatoes without pulling up the entire vine, and often they ate the tubers raw. The real harvest took place in late summer. Sweet potatoes had a good yield, and higher quality fruit, on poor, sandy soil, so this was an especially important crop for poorer farmers. But it made up a significant part of the diet of every class of southerner, including the planter and the slave. After the harvest, the fields were gleaned by hogs, and thus the sweet potato crop contributed to fattening the family's meat.

There were many varieties of sweet potato, including Spanish, Carolina, brimstone, purple, and red. There was even a "white" sweet potato known as the Bermuda. Sweet potatoes spoiled if they were frozen, so protected storage was essential. Most common was a hill of earth and decaying organic material such as was used for turnips. Some prosperous planters and farmers had potato houses, often partially underground, where potatoes were protected from ordinary freezing weather and where a fire could provide heat on arctic nights. Sweet potatoes, nutritious and loaded with vitamins, were well worth protecting. Most commonly they were baked in the ashes of the fireplace from which they could be raked out, peeled, and eaten piping hot. An oven, if available, was better, if for no other reason than that the potatoes came out cleaner. Often they were greased before baking to make them easier to peel. They could be sliced and then fried, or boiled and made into various dishes, including pies. A traveler in south-central Mississippi said that he "ate sweet potatoes with wild turkeys and various other meats, had a potato pie for dessert and roasted potatoes offered to him as a side dish, drank sweet potato coffee and sweet potato home brew, had his horse fed on sweet potatoes and sweet potato vines, and when he retired he slept on a mattress stuffed with sweet potato vines and dreamed that he was a sweet potato that someone was digging up."[3] However they were cooked, and no matter how often they were eaten, sweet potatoes were almost always good.[4]

The cowpea was only slightly less important than the sweet potato. In the antebellum South it was apparently more the custom to plant peas in the cornfields than in separate patches. In the New South, peas were an important hay crop and leguminous soil-builder before soybeans were planted widely, and they were sowed separately. A great many varieties were cultivated, including "small white," "lady peas," "cuckold's increase," "whippoorwills," and "britches and jacket," as well as the still familiar blackeye and crowder. Peas were best picked green, but they were still good food when picked after they had dried on the vine. One great advantage of dried peas was that they could be preserved for months; it was perfectly possible in the spring to eat peas that had been harvested the previous summer, but weevils ruined many plans for future pots of peas. Almost always, green or dry, they were boiled with fat pork or perhaps a ham hock; the dry peas had to be soaked overnight before cooking, or cooked much longer than green ones. They were nourishing; during the last dark winter of the Civil War, General Lee gave the lowly pea credit for preserving his army.[5]

The Irish potato, though native to the Western Hemisphere, was apparently brought to the southern colonies by the Scotch-Irish. Never as important as the sweet potato, it was basically a spring crop. The great disadvantage of Irish potatoes in the Old South was the fact that seed potatoes could not be preserved through the winter and had to be imported from the North each spring. When good water connections existed, as on the Mississippi and the East Coast, this was not an insurmountable problem, and the railroads when they came made seed potatoes available at other places; but the Irish potato lagged far behind the sweet potato in southern favor. The Irish method of preparation, boiling whole potatoes in the skin, was abandoned early, though new potatoes were often boiled whole with the skin largely scraped off rather than pared. More often, chunks of potato, like other vegetables, were boiled with some pork or pork grease. Once they were cooked, milk could be added, and the whole crushed together became mashed or creamed potatoes. Potato salad was probably made before the Civil War, but few if any references to it are to be found. Finally, the

Irish potato could be baked, and it was fried in hog lard like almost anything else.[6]

Almost every vegetable eaten in the South today was eaten before the Civil War. A surprising number of them, like the Irish and sweet potatoes, were of American origin. The peanut originated in South America, probably Brazil, was taken from there to Africa, then brought back to Virginia aboard slave ships. The tomato and the eggplant were American plants, and contrary to popular belief many southerners, including Thomas Jefferson and many New Orleanians, ate tomatoes before the Civil War. Before 1860, eggplant seems to have been used primarily, if not entirely, as an ornamental. Most of the beans planted in southern fields and gardens were American rather than European varieties. Especially favored were the common green bean, also called string bean and snap bean, and a small variety of the lima bean known to southerners as butter beans. White beans and red beans were planted, usually in a cornfield. In Louisiana and Texas, where French and Spanish influence was great, beans with rice and beans with chili peppers were especially enjoyed. Peppers, incidentally, were another product of the Western Hemisphere; they ranged from sweet or bell peppers to Mexican varieties that were hotter than the normal human mouth could stand. A soldier in the Mexican War brought back some pepper seed from Tabasco and gave some of them to the owner of Avery Island on the coast of Louisiana. He thus founded an industry that today ships millions of bottles of Tabasco sauce all over the nation.[7]

Many other vegetables were grown in gardens but seldom if ever in the fields. Green peas, usually called English peas, were an early spring vegetable. Pumpkins were not so highly regarded as farther north, but they were planted. Cabbage, beets, carrots, parsnips, lettuce, cucumbers, squash (a special favorite because it continued to bear in hot weather), okra, asparagus, radishes, onions, shallots, broccoli, artichokes, and rhubarb could be found. In most of the South the intense heat of midsummer, which enervated vegetables and gardeners but stimulated grass and weeds, tended to bring gardens to a sorry pass. Southerners obtained their best vegetables in spring and fall, and sometimes in midwinter they had more from stored turnips, sweet potatoes, and dry peas than they had in midsummer.[8]

Just as almost all families in small towns and many in the larger ones kept cows and chickens, so most townsmen made a vegetable garden. Slaves from nearby plantations and poorer farmers from the region brought vegetables into town for sale. Sometimes they peddled door to door, but more often they sold their entire load to a local merchant who then retailed to his customers. In the autumn northern ships brought vegetables into the major ports of the South, and these imports found a good market because southern gardens that had burned out during the summer had not yet begun bearing fall vegetables.[9]

Except in sparsely settled Florida and Texas and in southernmost Louisiana, the antebellum South produced little in the way of citrus fruits. Oranges in particular were much liked, however, and those who could afford them bought. They were deemed an especially appropriate gift for the sick. Bananas were imported into Charleston and New Orleans in great numbers, and coconuts were also familiar. Lemons seem to have been used almost entirely for flavoring drinks and pies; lemonade was a favorite wherever it was served.[10]

Apples and peaches thrived in the upper South, and peaches could be grown fairly near the Gulf. In fact, even though the fruit originated in Persia and was brought to the New World by the Spaniards, the first settlers in the Carolinas and Georgia found peaches under cultivation by the Indians. The "Indian peach," a small red-blushing cling fruit that apparently bred true from seed, was still common in the South after 1900. It was highly resistant to insects and fungus, and it was from this peach that brandy was distilled over much of the South down to the Civil War. Other varieties, some freestone, quickly followed. Apples came directly from England. They did best in the border states, especially in the Piedmont, the Appalachians, and the Great Valley; they could be grown successfully farther south, but they did not ripen to the rich red color brought on by early frosts. Apples were the basis for cider, a most popular drink that when well fermented and not yet turned to vinegar, might have up to 10 percent alcoholic content. Unlike Pennsylvanians, southerners seldom distilled cider into applejack. Both apples and peaches could be preserved by drying, and dried they were a favored winter dish. Other fruits encountered were grapes, figs, cherries, and, now and then, apricots. Watermelons and canteloupes were favored foods. Most of the time fruit was eaten raw, often with cream, but many housewives knew how to preserve fruits in sugar. Such preservation was not practiced widely because the earthen jars normally used were not as reliable as the patented glass jars that would be manufactured after the Civil War.[11]

Wild fruits and nuts continued to be a significant part of southern diet. Probably blackberries were the most-eaten wild fruit; they were delicious fresh, especially when served with cream, fine preserved, and they made good pies and good wine. Muscadines and scuppernongs (beginning to be cultivated) were good fresh from the vine and also made good preserves. Wild plums spread rapidly after the forests were cleared away, but they were eaten mainly by children. Persimmons were food for possums more than for people, but after a good frost they were sweet, or at least, two out of three were; the third was so astringent that the mouth remained puckered for minutes. Before the Civil War, forests were still full of delicious American chestnuts and the lesser chinquapins, and black walnuts and hickory nuts abounded. Pecans were being cultivated before mid-century, but they did not become an important commercial crop until much later. Cracking and eating nuts was one way to while away a long winter evening.[12]

In the upper South, maple trees afforded syrup and at times sugar. Now and then someone was lucky enough to find a bee tree; tracking bees back to the hollow tree where the honey was stored was a prized skill. In the eighteenth century, sugar had been very expensive; those who could afford to buy it all all bought a solid cone and shaved off what they needed with a knife. The cone was so precious that it was often kept under lock and key. By the mid-nineteenth century it had become comparatively cheap. Sugarcane was made into molasses in the eighteenth century, but the plant could not fully mature in the comparatively short growing season of the Gulf Coast, and it was not until 1796 that Etienne de Boré learned to crystallize brown sugar from Louisiana cane. Sorghum was grown in the upper South before the Civil War and made a rather sour molasses much inferior to that made from sugarcane. Overall, the people of the Old South did not use nearly so much sweetening as southerners of today, but they probably used more molasses. Children might get candy at Christmas, but they were unlikely to taste it any other time of year unless some relative liked to make candy. Fruit desserts were usually unsweetened; real sugar was saved for other desserts or for toddies.[13]

The middle-class American of today might find the diet of the ordinary family of the Old South somewhat Spartan, but compared with people in most other nations, southerners ate extremely well. Their food was loaded with calories—not far from five thousand a day. They could eat this amount only because they did so much hard physical labor. In many households there was not much variety, but this resulted at least as much from lack of imagination as from lack of food. So well did southerners eat that a newly arrived Irish immigrant was chided for prevaricating when he wrote home that he ate meat two times a day when he really ate it every meal. He excused himself on the grounds that nobody in Ireland would believe him if he claimed so much luxury.[14]

By the standards of the late twentieth century, the people of the Old South drank prodigious quantities of alcoholic beverages, so much so that it is easy to forget that they drank much of beverages less inspiring. Water, as was natural in the heat of a southern summer, was the most popular drink, and a spring or well of flavorsome water was something to be proud of. William Byrd's surveying party made a special stop at one John Ives', "for a drink of good water is as rare in these parts as good doctrine." Water was the usual table drink; foreign travelers noted that in most of the country, wine was seldom encountered at the table; whiskey drinkers often took water or something else nonintoxicating at dinner and did their heavy drinking later.[15]

Southerners drank large quantities of milk, though when a family was dependent upon its own cows, the amount might vary considerably from season to season. Some did produce milk in large quantities; fifty miles upriver from Savannah, William Bartram came upon a man whose slaves were milking forty cows.[16] Probably the milk was drunk by the slaves themselves, since they were so far from any market. As noted, southerners drank buttermilk and ate clabber. Finally, milk was almost a necessity for a family with small children.

Coffee and tea were widely drunk, though tea seems to have been more an upper-class beverage than was coffee. Travelers noted that Americans drank coffee and milk with their meals; southerners of the early nineteenth century, in fact, seem to have been as addicted to coffee as their descendants of today. The coffee beans were brought from a store or ordered through a factor, roasted at home, and pounded or ground as they were needed. Already in Louisiana the beans were roasted longer than elsewhere, and "dark roast" coffee astounded outsiders. When real coffee could not be had, substitutes, especially dried and roasted sweet potatoes, were used. Thus the South was prepared for at least one Civil War sacrifice.[17]

Apparently antebellum southerners never made beer or ale in large quantities. Considering the climate, and the popularity of beer in the modern South, this is difficult to understand. Some beer was brewed, of course, and some was imported, but it was not a popular drink. In fact, it seems to have been thought of as more medicinal than refreshing. Cider was popular, but it was available only a few months a year. Despite much propaganda, native wines were never very good; usually they were consumed from the crock in which they were made. Foreign wines were favored, but they were so expensive that ordinary people seldom tasted them.[18]

Until the Scotch-Irish brought the blessing of corn whiskey to America, rum was the most common spirit, imported from the West Indies or New England. Byrd said that the rum from New England was so bad that it was not improperly called "kill devil." Another distilled drink has attracted less attention. Thousands of southern acres were planted in peach trees, and the peaches were distilled into peach brandy. There was no export market for this product, so presumably it was drunk at home or, at least, in the neighborhood where it was distilled. As late as 1864 Sherman's foragers found tremendous quantities of peach brandy as they marched through Georgia.[19]

With the exception of south Louisianians, the people of the South continued to prefer the beneficial effects of corn whiskey to that of other forms of alcohol. Except perhaps for the addition of a little sugar and water to make a toddy, postfrontier generations continued to prefer their whiskey straight. Harriette Arnow found that the mint julep was mentioned in Nashville records for the first time in 1814, and she hazards the opinion that it was a drink for new arrivals, because the farmers of the Cumberland would have thought a man or woman who preferred the taste of mint to that of whiskey "a most curious person indeed." The whiskey barrel, or jug, continued to be essential to hospitality, and it played a role in militia musters, political campaigning, the celebration of special occasions—twenty-four toasts were drunk at Hillsboro, North Carolina, on the Fourth of July, 1823—and even at camp meetings.[20]

Not all this tremendous outpouring of liquor took place at home. Taverns, most of them of indifferent to terrible quality, were spaced out on the most frequently traveled roads, seven to ten miles apart. The bars were the busiest parts of these establishments because they served local customers as well as travelers. Perhaps drinkers went to the taverns because drinks were available there which were not available at home, but most seem to have ordered whiskey. One suspects that the tavern was a haven from the cares and annoyances of home, where a man could drink with other men rather than alone or with his wife. Customers, in other words, were attracted as much by company as by strong drink. As the antebellum years passed, more and more "groggeries," establishments whose sole business was selling liquor, came into being. Whether taverns and groggeries encouraged additional drunkenness, or whether it seemed so because drunks congregated around them, one cannot say, but it was widely believed that they added to the number of those who drank themselves into frenzy, stupor, or poverty.[21]

There can be little doubt that antebellum southerners drank too much. Temperance societies arose here and there, but they accomplished little. Protestant ministers often preached against intemperance, but even those who damned all strong drink might look upon wine and beer as healthful. Most people, in fact, looked upon moderate drinking of hard liquors as beneficial, and "moderate" before the Civil War would probably be considered "heavy" today. Not long after the Louisiana Purchase a young Creole woman in Opelousas, Louisiana, criticized American men because they were always willing to take another bottle, even though they were already drunk. She seems to have been a fairly accurate observer.[22]

The antebellum South boasted of its hospitality, and southerners were indeed a hospitable people. The ordinary southern farmer could not match the wealthy planter in the bounty he extended to his guests. He did, however, offer what he could, from the best bed in the house to a table loaded to the extent of his ability. Relatives and neighbors were the usual recipients of his hospitality; it might amount to nothing more than a meal, but it could, in the case of relatives, involve visits that lasted for months. Weddings were occasions for hospitality and joy making, and funerals, too, demanded hospitality. Probably, however, what southerners enjoyed most of all were "work frolics"—house-raisings, logrollings, corn shuckings, and the like. Most such frolics included a jug that circulated freely, and many ended in a dance, unless one of the stricter evangelical sects had convinced too many people of the neighborhood that dancing was sinful. Dancing, indeed, was such a delight that commercial balls were common even in the smaller towns, and they attracted the young and a remarkable proportion of the old from miles around.

Whatever southern hospitality meant, it did not mean the acceptance of any stranger who came down the road. The southern farmer, like the frontiersman, was likely to turn strangers away unless the hour was so late that they were obviously in distress. Even then, the householder almost always accepted a reasonable amount for bed and board; most would ask for their six bits or a dollar if the stranger did not offer it. Frederick Law Olmsted was convinced by 1860 that the whole idea of southern hospitality was so much humbug, but he also knew that if he had had letters of introduction and planned his route properly and that if his accent had been different, his reception would have been different.[23]

When the ordinary southerner did open his doors, he opened them wide. J. S. Buckingham, who had been discourteously treated near Athens, Georgia, received many invitations when he was in the Macon area—a locality damned by many other travelers—and was rescued when stranded between Jonesboro and Blountville in Tennessee. In Savannah he was impressed by the fact that there was so much visiting that a stranger who became known to one family quickly became known to others. Harriet Martineau found that hospitality was the most prominent characteristic of the "new society" she found around Montgomery, Alabama. John Abbott was impressed by his invitations to dine at the homes of hospitable friends in Mobile. Such experiences were perhaps not the norm, but they were too frequent to be overlooked.[24]

What the southerner, farmer or townsman, really enjoyed, however, was a gathering of family and friends at his home. This demanded a certain level of prosperity, but certainly not planter status. But one could not well entertain twenty or more people on salt pork, corn bread, and turnip greens. The food at such gatherings was not gourmet style; in fact, with the exception of New Orleans and possibly Charleston and Baltimore, the concept of fine food in the European sense hardly existed in the Old South. From the British yeoman, from the Indian, and from the frontier the southerner had inherited a preference for large amounts of different kinds of good food rather than a few dishes of presumably superb food. The host and his lady would, if possible, have pork, beef, game, and possibly fish; corn bread and wheat bread; three, four, or more kinds of vegetables; fruits if in season; and probably a dessert. To drink there would be water, coffee, milk, and almost surely whiskey. By modern standards quantity of the food prepared was enormous, and often the table could not seat more than a third or a half of those gathered. It is interesting that buffet service seems never to have been used to solve this problem. Rather the guests were assigned priorities by what amounted to rank, usually determined by age, which meant that children learned patience early in life; they often waited until the second or third table.[25]

Weddings probably offered the best opportunities for community merrymaking. In the rural South, weddings practically always were held in the home rather than in church; this was true even in Catholic south Louisiana well into the nineteenth century and continued after the Civil War.[26] The ceremony was, of course, in the bride's home, and it was held in the morning or at noon to allow time for the rest of the day's festivities. The groom's party gathered at his home and rode to the bride's. On the way they would "race for a bottle," and the winner passed his prize around so that everyone could have a drink. Thus they were in a mood for further celebration by the time they arrived.

The ceremony itself was seldom long, and it was followed in the early afternoon by a feast. On the frontier this feast had been mainly game, and the quantity depended upon the luck of the chase, but by the time farms and plantations were well established, all sorts of meats and vegetables in season went on the table. Then as now the bride's family took pride in the amount set forth. When the feast was over, and when a little time for digestion had passed, the dancing began and might continue until midnight. Before then, however, a group of the bride's friends had taken her and put her in bed, followed by a group of young men who installed the groom beside her. The next morning the wedding party (the women had slept in the house if there was room enough; the men went home or to neighbors' homes, or camped out in the woods) set forth to the groom's home for the "infare." Here another feast was provided. Incidentally, if the bride was a widow, the celebration would not be so elaborate, but the happy couple could expect a "shivaree," which at best would keep them awake; the revelers might enter the house and demand to be fed. In the upper South the shivaree was not so common; it seems to have been applied mostly to newlywed couples when they moved into their new home. Obviously, these southern wedding customs originated on the frontier. As the years passed, one feature after another fell into disuse—first the bottle race, then the infare, then the custom of putting the couple to bed. The wedding feast and dance did continue in many areas until after the Civil War, and the dance has not entirely disappeared today. This writer not long ago attended a wedding after which huge quantities of food and drink (party food and champagne, not hearty victuals and whiskey) were served to hundreds of people who then danced to the music of a Cajun band.[27]

For obvious reasons, the burial of the dead in the Old South could not be long delayed. On the frontier, where clergymen were scarce, the funeral might be held weeks, or even months, after burial. In later years, however, funeral and burial were scheduled as quickly as possible, often within twenty-four hours of death. Except in cities, funerals were almost always in the home, and, with the exception of Catholic south Louisiana, burial was as often in a family graveyard as in a churchyard. A funeral was obviously a sad occasion, but the solemnity was sometimes lost in the hospitality that the family of the deceased offered those who attended. Even the poorest family felt obligated to provide whiskey for those who sat up overnight with the corpse; in rural areas this custom, including the whiskey, persisted well into my lifetime. Those who were prosperous might spend a considerable amount on food and drink.[28]

Perhaps ordinary southerners had their most enjoyable hours at work frolics. These originated in the essential communal help of the frontier, but such activities did not end with the Indian wars. The clearing away of the South's forests continued through the nineteenth century and into the twentieth. My grandfather had been a mighty logroller in his day, the subject of proud and probably exaggerated tales by his contemporaries. House-raisings also persisted for generations; indeed, in special cases the people of a small southern town or rural community sometimes pool their skills today to raise a modest frame house.

The men who attended a logrolling or house-raising in the Old

South worked hard, fortified during the long day by baked sweet
potatoes and other comestibles prepared by the women. A drink of
whiskey now and then kept up morale. At the end of the work day,
something better and more substantial was the rule—a pot of burgoo or Brunswick stew, or perhaps a barbecued shoat or yearling
beef. Barbecue, which apparently originated in the West Indies,
became a favorite southern dish before the end of the colonial period and still has its devotees. At the work frolic the workers and
women, strength restored by food, were ready to dance into the
night. All they asked was a fiddler and a floor, or even a level piece
of ground. A wealthy Virginian who opened a new plantation in
Mississippi took twenty of his slaves to help a farmer neighbor
with his house-raising, but he was never asked to participate in
another.[29]

Corn shuckings were obviously useful, but they were not so essential as house-raisings or logrollings. Corn shucking was more
directly social in nature; it might be considered a form of harvest
celebration. A farmer who had brought in a large crop of corn
would announce a shucking for a certain evening; note that this
was a night party, not a daylight outing. In preparation he would
lay in a supply of drink—it could be whiskey, peach brandy, cider,
persimmon beer, or even, in later decadent years, bottled soda
pop—and food. He divided the corn in his barn loft into two equal
heaps. When the guests had gathered and were adequately re-
freshed, they chose sides and made a race out of shucking the two
piles of corn. Probably as much horseplay and courting went on as
working. It was necessary to have a referee, because a young man
who found a red ear of corn could kiss his choice of the girls, and
some were so unscrupulous as to bring several concealed red ears
with them. Some partook too freely of the jug and quietly went to
sleep among the shucks; other became quarrelsome, and it was
not uncommon for a cornshucking to turn into a bloody brawl. It
was not the usual practice for a corn shucking to turn into a dance,
but this certainly did happen at times.[30]

Despite the growing strictures of Baptist and Methodist ministers, most southerners before the Civil War continued to love mu-

sic and a hoedown. As towns grew in number, the commercial ball, promoted by the proprietor of a hotel or tavern for the sake of profit, became more and more common. J. S. Buckingham observed a dance near Wyer's Cave in Virginia and was shocked that so many of the young men were drunk. He also thought that the price, $2.50 per person with refreshments extra, was rather high. Southerners, however, did not think so. The giving of balls reached its height during the season in Charleston and during Mardi Gras in New Orleans, but small towns did not lag far behind. The people of rural Louisiana may have loved dancing even more than southerners elsewhere. Creoles were said to be fanatical on the subject, and "Acadian farm women, attired in cotton dress and barefooted, would dance at any chance they had. With several fiddlers to provide music and candles for light, Acadians of all ages would dance, eat gumbo, and drink a little tafia (a cheap rum) whenever the occasion provided." [31]

4

High on the Hog

EATING ON THE GREAT PLANTATION

The diet described in the preceding chapter was the diet of the majority of white people in the Old South. There was, however, an upper crust that ate a much greater variety and which served a greater quantity of food. In general, it would be a mistake to refer to this as "elegant" eating in the usual sense. A man like Thomas Jefferson, who had lived in Europe, might serve dinner "in the French style," and Dolly Madison had had enough experience in Washington to mix fine European dishes with American, but the usual "elegant" plantation meal was the "big eating" of the countryman carried to its logical extreme. This is not to imply that such eating was rude. On the contrary, the furniture was good, tablecloths were fine, and silver and china abounded; one planter's estate included more than five thousand dollars' worth of silverplate plus three dozen silver knives and forks and an abundance of china and pewter dishes and utensils. Tablecloths were plentiful, since forks were scarce and the cloths helped protect the table from dripping food, but they were of the best quality. The host and hostess were at least as much concerned with the variety and quantity of the food they offered as they were with the quality of any particular dish. This was not necessarily conspicuous consumption; the wealthy and aristocratic southerner took just as much pride as his less prosperous neighbor in seeing his guests eat heartily and abundantly.[1]

The fact that a man owned great tracts of land and many slaves did not necessarily mean that he set a sumptuous table. Planter families were a decided minority of the population, and only a minority of the planters built great houses where sumptuous meals could be served. Whether because of parsimony, lack of social ambition, good sense, or other reason, many a man who prospered continued to live in the double log cabin he had built when he settled on his place. In South Carolina and Georgia, plantation houses near the coast tended to be modest; after all, the family lived on the plantation only from late autumn or early winter into May. The rest of the year was spent in Charleston or Savannah, or traveling. If a Tidewater planter flaunted his wealth, it was more likely to be in his town house than on the land which made it possible. Incidentally, well-to-do families who lived year round in a town or city might set a table as luxurious as that of any planter.[2]

As on the farm and in the town, the most common breakfast food on the plantation was fried pork, preferably ham or bacon, served with eggs if they could be had, and washed down with coffee. Much milk was drunk, clabber was eaten, and grits were commonly served. G. W. Featherstonhaugh, who breakfasted with John C. Calhoun at the statesman's Fort Hill Plantation, reported "excellent coffee with delicious cream, and that capital, national dish of South Carolina, snow white hominey [grits] brought hot to table . . . which ought always to be eaten with lumps of sweet fresh butter buried in it." Another visitor to South Carolina had rice, eggs, and cocoa for breakfast, and the Yankee bride of a North Carolina planter was impressed by the great variety of hot cakes, waffles, and biscuits on the breakfast table. One Nashville Christmas breakfast, almost certainly unusual, consisted of pork sausage, baked spare ribs, quail, grits, wheat bread, biscuits, chocolate, and milk.[3]

William Howard Russell, visiting the Roman plantation in south Louisiana in 1861, had coffee and biscuits, then rode over the plantation. When he returned to the house about nine, breakfast proper was served, including "strange dishes of tropical origin. There was the old French abundance, the numerous dishes and efflorescence of napkins, and the long-necked bottles of Bordeaux, with a steady current of pleasant small talk." A day or two later at the Burnside estate he had fish, shrimp, and beef to start the day. Beefsteak, fried, of course, was an accepted southern breakfast long before it became a western brag. Fish also were enjoyed as well at breakfast as at any other meal.[4]

Dinner was the main meal on the plantation as well as in the yeoman farmer's house, but in the mansion it usually was served later in the day. The time varied from household to household and even from day to day within the same household, but three o'clock in the afternoon would seem to have been the most common time. Probably there was a tendency for people to go to the table earlier as the years passed and the antebellum period drew toward its tragic end.

The North American plantation originated in Virginia, and good foods became a part of that province's tradition in the early colonial years. In 1634 a visitor to Jamestown reported that the most prosperous Virginians set their tables with turkey, geese, capon, chickens, and other fowl, as well as with pork and kid. Almost two hundred years later a northern student visiting the great Carter mansion, Shirley, reported that his host's family and guests came together at one o'clock, the men to drink rum and the women to chat. Dinner was served at three.

> Mrs. Carter ladles soup at one end of the table, while her husband carves a saddle of mutton at the other. Black boys hand around dishes of ham, beef, turkey, duck, eggs and greens, sweet potatoes, and hominy. After a round of champagne the upper cloth is removed, and upon the damask beneath plum pudding, tarts, ice cream, and brandied peaches are served. When you have eaten this, off goes the second table cloth, and then upon the bare mahogany table is set the figs, raisins, and almonds, and before Mr. Carter is set two or three bottles of wine—Madeira, port, and a sweet wine for the ladies—he fills his glass and pushes them on.[5]

Another traveler in antebellum Virginia noted that the Virginians did not eat terrapin, like the Marylanders to the north, but that "a chine [backbone], jole [jowl], or ham or bacon, embedded with greens about it, are standard dishes." He also noted that Virginians were fond of sturgeon above other fish. Frederick Law

Olmsted, who found few things in the South to approve, praised
two dinners he ate at lesser plantations in Virginia. At one he had
"fried fowl, and fried bacon and eggs, and cold ham; there were
preserved peaches, and preserved quinces and grapes; there was
hot wheaten biscuit, and hot short cake and hot corn cake, and hot
griddle cakes, soaked in butter; there was coffee, and there was
milk, sour or sweet, whichever I preferred to drink." At the other
plantation house he had relays of hot corn bread "of an excellence
quite new to me." No other bread was served, and "but one vegetable . . . sweet potato, roasted in ashes, and this, I thought, was the
best sweet potato also that I ever had eaten; but there were four
preparations of swine's flesh, besides fried fowls, fried eggs, cold
roast turkey, and o'possum, cooked, I know not how, but it somehow resembled baked suckling pig. The only beverages on the
table were milk and whiskey."[6]

Rich South Carolina planters matched their peers in Virginia in
the opulence of their tables; one gets the impression that seafoods
were more important in the Palmetto State, though this is not necessarily correct. Still, people who could invent such dishes as she-
crab soup and shrimp pie must have had a special affinity for the
bounty of the sea. Some even tried to keep saltwater fish in cap-
tivity, but otters, crabs, and alligators defeated these efforts. Meals
in Charleston or Beaufort were at least as good and as sumptuous
as those on the plantations; the oven in one Charleston home held
half a beef and six turkeys at one time. John Grimball tells of a
meal for eight in Charleston that consisted of two kinds of soup,
turkey served with oyster sauce, ham, venison, mutton, wild ducks,
turtle, vegetables, custards, apple pudding, bread, and cheese. The
most elaborate dish encountered anywhere by this writer was a
Charleston "preserve of fowl"; this consisted of a dove stuffed into
a quail, the quail into a guinea hen, "the hen into a duck, the duck
into a capon, the capon into a goose, and that in turn into a pea-
cock or turkey, and so roasted and cut into transverse sections."[7]
On the Alston plantation Grimball ate at least as well as in the city.

> The table was set with turtle soup at each end [and] two parallel
> dishes, one containing a leg of boiled mutton and the other turtle

steaks and fins. Next was a pile of Maccaroni in the center of the table, and on each side of it was a small dish of oysters. Next were two parallel dishes corresponding with the two above mentioned, one of them with turtle steaks and fins, the other a boiled ham. When the soups were removed, their place was supplied at one end by a haunch of venison, and at the other by a roast turkey . . . [A second course included] bread pudding . . . jelly . . . a high glass dish of ice cream . . . [and] a pie. . . . [Then came] two high baskets . . . one of bananas and the other of oranges. One larger of apples.

During and after this orgy of food, Madeira, sherry, champagne, and liquors were drunk.[8]

A dinner for Felix Robertson in Nashville in 1837 consisted of a rich soup with rice; "two very large boiled fishes, elegantly cooked and served with creamed Irish potatoes, bread, and pickles"; boiled ham; roast beef; winter vegetables; pickles made of mangoes, watermelon rind, and cucumbers; and apple pie, custard pie, cakes and jellies for dessert. Only coffee, tea, and milk were to be had to drink. The Charles Colcock Jones family of Georgia ate much beef and mutton as well as the ever present fresh and cured pork. The Joneses also ate large quantities of seafood when visiting their rice plantation, and they enjoyed imported spices and tropical fruits. Mrs. Isaac Hilliard, Arkansas sister-in-law of Bishop Leonidas Polk, noted in her diary that after the men of her household had accepted an invitation to eat game at a neighboring plantation, the ladies who stayed at home made do with gumbo, turkey, a young rooster, and beef tongue, plus vegetables, pickles, guava jelly, plum pudding, and syllabub.[9]

Harriet Martineau, visiting a plantation near Montgomery, Alabama, in the spring, had a light lunch at eleven, then dinner at two—"now and then soup (not good), always roast turkey and ham, a boiled fowl here, a tongue there; a small piece of nondescript meat, which generally turns out to be pork disguised; hominy, rice, hot corn bread, sweet potatoes; potatoes mashed with spice, very hot, salad and radishes, and an extraordinary variety of pickles." She did not like the way one was expected to eat "everything with everything else. If you have turkey and ham on your plate, you are requested to add tongue, pork, hominy, and pickles. Then succeed pies of apple, squash, and pumpkin . . . and a variety of preserves as extraordinary as the preceding pickles. . . . These are almost all from the West Indies." Nor was this all. "Dispersed about the table are . . . almonds, raisins, hickory, and other nuts; and to crown the whole, large blocks of ice cream." Martineau noted that champagne was abundant and cider frequent. "Ale and porter may now and then be seen, but claret is the most common drink."[10]

Great plantations serving gargantuan meals were to be found in every state, though they were apparently not so abundant west of the Appalachians. A northern bride wrote of her husband's family and neighbors in North Carolina: "There must always be two or three different kinds of meats on . . . [the] table. . . . [And] I believe they esteem above all dishes . . . roasted pig dressed with red pepper and vinegar. Their bread is corn bread . . . & biscuit with shortening and without anything to make them light and beaten like crackers. The bread and biscuit are always brought to the table hot." Thomas Dabney, a Virginian removed to Mississippi, fattened sheep until some of them suffocated; the sacrifice was worth it to assure the quality of his remaining mutton. In order that his beef might be suitable to his estate he worked steers as oxen for two years, then fattened them for two years before they were slaughtered. His pigs were so fat that their tails always curled, leading some neighbors to think that they were a special breed.[11]

Supper was light on the plantation as it was on the farm or in town. Dolly Madison's guests went to their rooms at ten and servants brought them a light supper. The supper at Carter's Shirley plantation was also light, and followed by a nightcap. Henry Bernard, visiting in Beaufort, South Carolina, was served strawberries with rich cream and white sugar in the evening. Harriet Martineau observed that planters' families sometimes sat around the table in the evening, but that more commonly a tray was handed around and the guests took plates, which they held on their laps. Tea or coffee was drunk with waffles, ham, beef, and cake. Somewhat later, just before going to bed, guests were offered cake and wine.[12]

Obviously, antebellum planters consumed a great deal of alcoholic beverages. Even the Reverend Charles Colcock Jones, bitter enemy of drunkenness, drank port wine and beer for medicinal purposes. The chief difference in drinking habits between the planter's family and the farmers was that the planter was much more likely to serve and partake of imported wines. Practically all kinds were used, but Madeira and claret seem to have been favored over all others; perhaps the greater alcoholic content of Madeira gave it a special appeal. The planter was also likely to use imported brandy and other liqueurs that would seldom if ever appear in a farmer's home. Eggnog was a great favorite, especially at Christmas time, though there were those then as now who regarded it as a tragic waste of eggs and whiskey.[13]

Planters did, of course, serve hard liquor, usually whiskey, but they were less likely to serve it unadulterated. They might prepare a toddy like that of the farmer, make eggnog, or have a punch. As legend has it, the mint julep was a favorite concoction, sometimes made with brandy rather than whiskey. While visiting the Burnside plantation upriver from New Orleans, William Howard Russell learned that the julep was "a panacea for all the evils of climate." The slave detailed to serve him brought him one early in the morning to help him with his bath. Hardly was the first one finished when another arrived, strongly recommended because "fever very bad this morning—much dew." The height of something or the other came one morning when the servant brought a third glass, declaring emphatically, "Massa says, sir, you had better take this, because it'll be the last he make before breakfast." One suspects that the average plantation host served his guests far more alcohol than he took himself. Several strong drinks before breakfast may have been pleasant, but they did not leave the manager of a busy plantation the energy and acumen he needed for his business.[14]

Of the hospitality of the planters and well-to-do townsmen of the Old South there can be no doubt; the witnesses are too abundant. The story of the lonesome lord of many acres who at rifle point forced passersby to partake of his hospitality is probably apocryphal, but it does make the point that life on a plantation could be isolated and lonely; the visit of a well-informed traveler could be a much-welcomed break in the routine of the seasons. A statesman 'or otherwise famous or distinguished man, a stranger who came with letters of introduction from friends, neighbors, and above all relatives, could be assured of a warm welcome.

Much of General Washington's time during the Revolution was taken up with entertaining officers from abroad, some distinguished, others wishing to become distinguished, who visited his headquarters. The general set an ample table: eight or ten large dishes, then a second course of pastries, and a final course of apples and nuts, with enough wine for numerous toasts. It might be interesting to know what the rations of the men in the Continental Line were at the same time. William Bartram was well enough known to be cordially received in Georgia. He noted that on one rice plantation he was entertained "in every respect as a worthy gentleman could a stranger. . . . I spent the evening very agreeably and the day following (for I was not permitted to depart sooner.)" In Charleston General James Wilkinson was elaborately entertained by Mrs. Thomas Radcliffe. The guests danced until eleven, when oyster patties were served. Next the gentlemen were served a supper of beefsteak and cold turkey, after which the dancing continued until two o'clock in the morning. One unusual aspect of this affair was that the general provided a military band.[15]

Travelers fortunate enough to be welcomed into southern planters' homes spoke highly of southern hospitality. Bishop Henry B. Whipple reported that "The people of the southern states are generally much more hospitable than northerners." Charles Augustus Murray remained at a Virginia plantation "four or five days; and if the wishes of the friendly and excellent host . . . had been alone to be consulted I might have remained there as many weeks." Sir Charles Lyell noted that "they alone who have traveled in the southern states, can appreciate the ease and politeness with which a stranger is made to feel himself at home."[16]

But Whipple, Murray, and Lyell were, of course, distinguished men. Despite some claims, hospitality was not extended to all who came to the gates. The Reverend Charles Colcock Jones, a man himself of considerable distinction, had known Henry Clay. Several years after the Kentuckian's death, Jones called at Clay's Ashland plantation, where Clay's son and family lived, only to be told by a fat Irishwoman that Mr. Clay was away from home and that Mrs. Clay was unwell. Isaac Weld, after being assured in Washington that he would be welcomed by any planter in Virginia, crossed the Potomac and as night approached went to a plantation nearby; there he was roughly informed that there was a tavern down the road. More hospitable Virginians, when they heard of this event, explained that the owner of the plantation concerned had but recently bought it and that being a Scotsman he could hardly be expected to know how to behave. In North Carolina, General Jeremiah Slade was well received when he sought shelter at a well-appointed plantation, but when he was ready to leave the next morning he was presented with a bill.[17]

Weddings were as much an occasion for celebration among the gentry as among the common people. George Washington's wedding was to a widow, and a wealthy one; at the celebration in her home the guests were amply wined and fed hams, oysters, beef and pork roasts, jams, jellies, fruitcakes, and pies. The knot was tied at Christmas, which perhaps explains the absence of vegetables. Letitia M. Burwell noted that preparations for a wedding included "the liveliest egg-beating, butter-creaming, raisin-stoning, sugar-pounding, egg-frothing, waffle-making, pastry-baking, jelly-straining, silver-cleaning, floor-rubbing, dress-making, hair-curling, lace washing, ruffle-crimping, tarlatan-smoothing, trunk-moving—guests arriving, servants running, girls laughing." She remembered that the guests generally arrived a week or two before the ceremony and stayed often for a week afterward, "being accompanied by quite an army of Negro servants." When Betsy Worrell was married in Maryland, "between fifty and sixty people were present at the ceremony, who danced till 4 o'clock. . . . They kept up the Ball until Monday and then went to Middle Neck, accompanied by six carriages well filled. The bride and groom led the van in a new phaeton." Dick Hardaway Eggleston, whose plantation was near Woodville, Mississippi, gave a dinner and party for one hundred people in honor of a recently married couple.[18]

Perhaps the number of people entertained by planter families is the most impressive item to modern husbands and wives. The Egglestons, mentioned above, had sixty-one guests during January of 1830, some for only one meal, others for one or more nights. They had almost as many in September of the same year, during the busy harvest season. A century earlier William Byrd was inviting four to ten people home to dinner after church each Sunday, but he eventually noted in his diary that he had halted this practice because "we would not make our people work too much of a Sunday."[19] This would have been small potatoes to Martha Washington, whose recipe for making a cake began with "Take forty eggs . . ." Another former president's wife, Dolly Madison, wrote from Montpelier: "[We] had ninety persons to dine with us at one table—put up on the lawn." While Rachel lived, Andrew Jackson thoroughly enjoyed guests at the Hermitage. Henry A. Wise was greeted cordially, but General Jackson "gave us clearly to understand that he took no trouble to look after any but his lady guests; as for the gentlemen, there was the parlor, the dining room, the library, the sideboard and its refreshments; there were the servants, and if anything was wanting, all that was necessary was to ring."[20]

Katherine Du Pre Lumpkin wrote of her forbears that "more than anything else, they and their kinsmen visited among each other." Spontaneity characterized much of the hospitality of the planter class of the Old South. One Virginia couple had no children, and company was in part a substitute. Always at dinner the wife set places for those she expected and for six more "in case . . . [her husband] should meet friends and acquaintances, while riding over his plantation or in the neighborhood, whom he wished to ask home with him to dinner." Thomas Dabney "once had an Episcopal clergyman and his family, consisting of his wife, five children, and two servants to spend six weeks at Burleigh [Dabney's plantation]. When a Louisiana gentleman expressed a desire to establish a school near Raymond . . . [Dabney] received his family into his house, and they were entertained there for two months. This family consisted of the father and mother, their eight children and an adopted child, one Negro and four Irish servants, and two horses." Perhaps the height of spontaneity came when a young Georgia couple invited new friends, a husband and wife, to dine with them on Saint Simon's Island. This foursome found one another so congenial that a boat was sent fifteen miles for the visitors' baggage. They continued to enjoy one another's company so much that the visitors remained until two children had been born to them.[21]

The incessant visiting characteristic of the antebellum South was an important ingredient of the cement that bound the ruling class of the region together socially, intellectually, and, in time, politically. Letitia Burwell recalled that at a certain house one was sure of meeting "pleasant people from Virginia, Baltimore, Florida, South Carolina, and Kentucky, with whom the house was filled from May till November."[22] There were hundreds of other such houses, from Texas to Maryland and from Florida to Missouri, where the people who decided the destiny of their sections met and helped determine one another's opinions. The young people danced and courted, laughed and gossiped; and the women no doubt engaged in a little matchmaking when it was appropriate. But men, over toddies, mint juleps, or imported wines, became more and more convinced of the superiority of things southern, and of the necessity to resist to the death any Yankee attempts to bring about changes.[23]

It was a pleasant life. John A. Quitman wrote: "We hunt, ride, fish, pay morning visits, play chess, read or lounge until dinner. . . . In two hours afterward everybody—white and black—has disappeared. The whole household is asleep. . . . It is an indolent, yet charming life, and one quits thinking and takes to dreaming." It was in fact a hard life for women. Quitman wrote of one hostess that "the whole aim of this excellent lady appears to be to make others happy. . . . She is growing old, but her parlor is constantly thronged with the young and gay, attracted by her cheerful and never-failing kindness." It was also an expensive way of life. Jefferson was not the only southerner whose hospitality contributed to his bankruptcy.[24]

Undoubtedly the planter's hospitality was the slave's drudgery, though we have no records of the black people's thoughts on the subject. But it was a way of life dependent upon them. Southerners would continue to be hospitable after the ravages of the Civil War, but the almost grotesque abundance of upper-class entertainment was no longer possible. No doubt some very proper moral lessons are to be drawn from this, but one suspects that many white southerners, and a few blacks who have been caught up in the myth, would go back to the groaning tables of the Old South. There they would be surrounded by tall and slender young gentlemen who whisper into the ears of wasp-waisted and beautiful girls, the whole company waited upon by smiling black servitors and presided over by a host of Jovian dignity but understanding smile and his striking gray-haired spouse. She would still be beautiful after bearing a dozen children and devoting her life to the happiness of those children and the contentment of her husband. All of them would be immortal yet, despite the fact that their mortality was so soon to be so tragically proved.

5

Grease, Bedbugs, and Good Food

EATING AWAY FROM HOME IN THE OLD SOUTH

The antebellum southerner did not care for commercial hospitality. When it was necessary for him to travel, he much preferred to stop along the way with friends and relations. But this was not always possible, and in Charleston, Mobile, or New Orleans he might enjoy a private room and the hotel dining room. In rural areas and small towns, however, he found taverns that were indifferent at best, and too often terrible; at times the traveler might be forced to seek shelter with private families who supplemented whatever other income they might have by taking in strangers. This was true in other sections, too, but that fact did not improve conditions in the South. Diaries of native southerners, northerners, and foreign travelers are full of references to the accommodations they endured. Upper-classs southerners often took a vacation during July and August, after the crops had been laid by and before the harvest began. A few of the wealthy went north to New England or Saratoga, but most remained in the South. Resorts, usually boasting some kind of curative waters, were scattered over the region. New Orleanians might merely cross Lake Pontchartrain to the pine flats of southeast Louisiana, and others went to places as near home, but the more fashionable resorts were in the Appalachians, and White Sulphur Springs in Virginia was the most fashionable spa of all.

Except in the cities, and there to a much more limited degree than one might imagine, antebellum southerners simply did not "eat out" in the modern sense. Indeed, the word *restaurant* is of

French origin and did not come into use in France until well into the eighteenth century. Establishments that existed in order to provide full meals to the public in the sense that restaurants do today were rare in the Old South. Oyster bars and the like were available, but most eating places were operated in conjunction with lodging, and guests ate common fare from a common table. When a man went to such a place near his home, he was probably more interested in convivial drinking than in food. He was accompanied by his family only if the whole family was on the move in an area where he and his wife were strangers.

Roadside taverns, either in the country or in small towns, were too often the business of those who had failed in one or more other occupations. It was said that adventuresome Irishmen, wandering Frenchmen, and Englishmen who had left home for the good of all concerned often became tavern keepers. Gossip said that the Irishman was almost sure to serve plenty, however poor its quality. The Frenchman was reputed to serve much poor wine and to boast of how good his indifferent food was. The Englishman had a tendency to lie about his world travels as he carved away and spilled gravy on his guests. Virginians west of the mountains, felled by financial mismanagement or bad fortune, might turn successfully to tavern keeping. Joseph Baldwin tells of one who, after losing his slaves through endorsing a friend's note, turned his home into a tavern and kept everything exactly as it was except that he now charged for his hospitality. He and his family were as happy as ever. Finally, many taverns were operated by widows; this was one of the few ways in which a respectable woman could support herself.[1]

If there was any improvement in roadside accommodations and fare between the colonial period and the Civil War, it certainly was not universal. George Washington, surveying in the Shenandoah Valley, lived with "barbarians." He slept before the fire "upon a little hay, straw, fodder or bearskin . . . with man, wife, and children, like a parcel of dogs and cats." In 1861 William Howard Russell, on his way from New Orleans to the East Coast, noted that "it was a relief to get out of the train for a few minutes" at Holly Springs,

Mississippi, "where the passengers breakfasted at a dirty table on most execrable coffee, corn bread, rancid butter, and very dubious meat."[2]

Some of the most fervent lines penned by diarists pertained to taverns, and they seem to have been almost as bad in one part of the South as in another. In the late eighteenth century a traveler in the area of the great Dismal Swamp complained that nothing was to be had but "rancid fish, fat salt pork, and bread made of Indian corn." Later, in the Shenandoah Valley, he concluded that bad bacon, fried, and "sallad," the latter dressed with "the melted fat which remains in the frying pan" was the only food to be had in taverns. A Virginian, after paying seventy-five cents for supper and lodging near Charleston, now in West Virginia, reported "poor accommodations, bad attendance, and plenty of dirt." Harriet Martineau ate at a Virginia roadhouse that served bread, coffee, butter, eggs, ham, and steak, but found it all too sour to eat. J. S. Buckingham, one of the most critical of British travelers, complained that the inn on the road between Abingdon and Virginia Springs, and the fat colonel who kept it, were both extremely dirty, but he conceded that he got a better meal than he had expected. Buckingham's worst aesthetic experience in Virginia seems to have been near Wythe Court House where, after a bug-haunted night, he saw "a large house dog being sent in chase of a chicken, which he caught in his mouth and brought to the cook who forthwith killed, plucked, dissected, and fried the same for our use."[3]

Buckingham did find some good food, and much more often in Virginia than farther south. Near Abingdon he had excellent mutton, poultry, and vegetables, and at Fairfield he luxuriated in roast beef and veal, good vegetables, and wheaten bread. At Old Point Comfort he enjoyed a fine fish dinner of sheepshead and croaker. Buckingham understood one problem of the roadside tavern. Because bread was always served hot, and because cold meats were not ordinarily kept on hand in a warm climate, rapid service was impossible. Even with haste, it took an hour to get a meal on the table. Another Englishman, G. W. Featherstonhaugh, noted that travelers were likely to fare better in general farming areas where farmers gave more attention to wheat, butter, milk, and eggs than they did in cotton-growing country.[4]

The Carolinas were certainly no improvement over Virginia. In 1837 a Methodist minister complained that from Tarboro, North Carolina, to the Tennessee line he was served nothing except fried pork, eggs, and coffee. At Orangeburg, South Carolina, Sidney Andrews found the bread and biscuit both heavy and sour and the meat swimming in strong fat. At the same village Buckingham was served water in an unwashed glass that smelled of rum. Another traveler, near Georgetown, found the tavern keeper's family all sick with malaria, but after an hour's wait he was served bad coffee, bread, bacon, and butter that resembled axle grease thickened with salt.[5]

What was bad in the Carolinas became worse as the traveler moved westward. Central and western Georgia had especially villainous inns. Colonel William Gray, a Virginian, described a tavern at Milledgeville as "the vilest, dirtiest place that I have ever seen." At Columbus he found "another vile, dirty place, where we got a poor supper. All the taverns that I have seen in Georgia, except at Augusta, are execrable." To the north and east in the same state Buckingham was greatly outraged by bedbugs, "the largest, blackest, and most voracious kind," but he was even more upset with the "custom of the country" that placed the "driver of the barouche, the driver of the wagon, and our own white servants" at the table with his family. His temper was not improved at Macon, where "the table was miserably furnished; the beds dirty and ill provided." Another traveler near Columbus complained when he was offered pigs' feet, bacon in molasses, milk, and bread, all to be washed down with whiskey.[6]

Food did not improve to the westward. A lady who recorded her experiences may have been slightly gratified to get steak and gravy rather than pork to go with the whiskey she was served at breakfast, but only slightly. William Gray said that a good dinner was "a thing seldom met with in Mississippi." Served by the wife of a Methodist minister, "a very slattern in dress and person," he ate badly fried pork and eggs but good corn bread, and drank milk and bad coffee. Having had no supper he "ate heartily, though the table cloth was so foul that under other circumstances it would have spoiled my meal."[7]

The traveler was no better off in Louisiana, where outside of New Orleans even the best taverns were said to be miserable. A wealthy Monroe family returning from a visit to Kentucky had to ride horseback from Lake Providence, and had to sleep thirteen to the room on the way. A. A. Parker was discomfited when he could get only bread and meat at a place west of Natchitoches, but he was made more uncomfortable by the mulatto children of his host and his black consort. William Gray got a good dinner at Rees Perkins' ferry across the Calcasieu River, but when he spent the night at the house of Arsen Le Blue Comarsec [sic], a man with a Virginia-born wife and said to be worth $100,000, he was somewhat put out by the fact that there was no sugar for the coffee, no butter, and only sour milk, even though the host boasted of having over one thousand calves. Gray slept upon the floor where fleas attacked him voraciously.[8]

Arkansas and Texas, as might be expected from their frontier status, afforded the worst accommodations of all. We read of an inn proprietor in Arkansas who was "a mass of unsolid humanity, about two hundred and fifty [pounds] . . . kept moist by whiskey. . . . He was red-faced, bottle-nosed, and double-chinned, and . . . as he waddled about . . . he was followed by swarms of flies." Parker, Olmsted, and Gray especially deplored the lodging and eating in Texas. Perhaps the worst was described by Gray as a one-room frame house, "a wretchedly made establishment, and a blackguard rowdy set lounging about. The host's wife and children and about thirty lodgers, all slept in the same apartment, some in beds, some on cots, but the greater part on the floor. The supper consisted of fried pork and coarse corn bread and miserable coffee."[9]

There were honorable exceptions to the rule that rural and small-town taverns and inns were miserable places serving miserable food. John Melish found grits most delectable at an inn in eastern Georgia, and Isaac Weld reported excellent breakfasts in

Maryland. Even the hypercritical Buckingham found a fine "hotel" at Pendleton, South Carolina. When the Thomas Dabney family was moving to Mississippi in the 1830s they were well received and well fed by the people of Tennessee with whom they lodged at night. Charles Colcock Jones, Jr., who had been at college in the North, was delighted with a place about ten miles from Louisville that fed him hot biscuits, corn bread, eggs, fried chicken, and milk, all prepared in what he regarded as true southern fashion. Thirty miles west of Natchez, A. A. Parker found a good house kept by good people who gave him an excellent supper, and just inside Texas he had another good supper of venison, sweet potatoes, corn bread, coffee, and milk. Colonel Gray, who was almost as critical as English travelers, reported a fine supper that included milk and hominy at Fort Jessup, an excellent dinner of bacon, turnip greens, boiled eggs, corn bread, coffee, and milk near Washington, Texas, fine buttermilk and Texas blackberries on another occasion, and a good supper of wild turkey, stewed apples, milk, and coffee on still another.[10] But it must be admitted that the good meals were the exception.

The river steamer has become part of the myth of the Old South. Varina Howell Davis remembered, as the end of the nineteenth century drew near, that "The steam-boats were literally floating palaces of ease and luxury. I have never seen any hotel where the food was so exquisitely prepared or the provision of dainties so great." Mrs. Davis' father was a very wealthy man, and her husband was a prominent politician whose relatives, at least, were wealthy. Presumably she traveled on the best boats, and probably her memories of better days made those days seem even better than they were.[11] No contemporary travelers, native or foreign, went into ecstasies over steamboat fare, though many of them did comment favorably. Just as many more, however, wrote of bad food badly served. Apparently the steamboat menu was like that of southern homes in that it placed most emphasis on the quantity of food available and the largest possible number of items. On a good craft, most southerners would at least be content with their fare, but a foreigner who disliked southern food and southern manners might be highly critical. The foreigners, who were seeing something new, gave the best descriptions.

Sir Charles Lyell wrote that cabin passengers dined first, white nurses, children, and ship's officers second, white deck passengers (the least expensive ticket) third, white waiters fourth, and black passengers, free or slave, and black waiters last.[12] Buckingham gave a nose in the air description of the service.

> The principal dishes are taken off the table and carved or hacked on a sideboard by the negro stewards, who load the plates with so great a quantity of everything asked for, and so bury the whole in gravies and sauces, that it required a very strong appetite to conquer the repugnance which it creates. No delicacy is observed in the mode of carving, serving, or helping the guests. . . . Puddings are usually handed around in small white saucers, instead of plates, with a spoon in each, and nothing is refused. Everyone seems to think it a duty to accept and be thankful for whatever is set before him, and appears to exercise no more power of rejection or refusal than children at school.[13]

The dishes were the same as those served ashore, though apparently the better steamers served a smaller proportion of pork than the tavern or the second-class hotel. Ham was a standard dish, but so were roast beef, turkey, and other fowl. A steamer leaving New Orleans would offer turtle soup, waterfowl in season, shrimp, oysters, and other seafood, items that probably were not to be had on a ship departing downriver from Pittsburgh, Louisville, or Saint Louis. Vegetables were the standard ones because no others were to be had at the vessel's ports of call. The better boats served good wine, and presumably wine of some kind was available on good, bad, and indifferent craft. It was noticeable, however, that strong drink at the bar was more sought after than claret, Madeira, or other wines at the table.

The rapidity with which southerners and presumably all other Americans except perhaps a few from the effete Northeast ate their food was impressive. Buckingham noted that gentlemen waited for ladies to sit before seating themselves but that they then gulped down their dinner in ten minutes or less and walked away from the table still chewing. Eating with a knife was apparently universal. Buckingham was also concerned with the fact that coffee cups were almost always filled to overflowing, slopping into the saucer. He said that Americans solved this problem by drinking out of the saucers. Observers from other lands obviously did not understand that pouring coffee into the saucer was a common-sense method of cooling it without having to wait too long. But the American habit that disgusted outsiders the most, on steamboats, in taverns, in ballrooms, and almost everywhere was the enthusiasm with which southern men chewed tobacco and then spat it forth as they would. Ladies' gowns, extending to the floor as they did, were in constant jeopardy.[14] However, a not inconsiderable number of ladies dipped snuff, which necessitated some spitting on their part.

Vacations for clerks and factory workers may have come into being with the twentieth century, but upper-class southerners were great patronizers of resorts, most of them more accurately described as watering places, throughout the antebellum period. Many of the passengers on steamboats bound upriver in the late spring and early summer were Louisianians and Mississippians on their way to springs in Kentucky, Tennessee, or the North. People seldom openly went to such resorts purely in search of enjoyment; nearly every such spa made much of its medicinal waters. Back-country people began medicinal use of the springs in the Shenandoah Valley before the middle of the eighteenth century. Some three or four hundred such places existed at one time or another before the Civil War, though by 1861 some had long been out of business. In addition to the curative effect of the springs, some southerners were undoubtedly seeking relief from heat or disease plaguing coastal areas. A family might go no farther from New Orleans than to Ocean Springs or to Mandeville, but many Mississippi Valley families went to Newport or Saratoga. Kentucky's most famous resort was at Harrodsburg Springs, but there were dozens of others, including one at Mammoth Cave. Tennessee did not lag far behind Kentucky; Alabama had more than a dozen resorts; Georgia had as many, most of them near the Tennessee line;

and others were to be found in the western part of the Carolinas.[15]

Most of these resorts resembled one another. They advertised the curative properties of their waters, and many of them had physicians on hand to advise their guests. Their main purpose, however, was to provide a change of scene for their patrons and to bring together people from different areas. Buckingham visited a number of spas from South Carolina northward. After a day spent at Table Rock, North Carolina, he offered the following description. Some of the guests, he said, were there for health, and some for pleasure.

> And these were said to include some members of the first families in Carolina. Yet the place appeared to possess . . . no . . . attraction but that of climate. . . . The bed-rooms were dark and dingy, the bedding coarse and dirty; no wash stands, dressing-tables, mats or carpets; broken looking glasses, tallow candles, brass and tin candlesticks, and filthy negro servants. . . . . The dining rooms were not more than eight feet high . . . like a badly built soldier's barracks; and the fare was like that of nearly all the country inns, coarse, greasy, tough, badly dressed, and cold. . . . Yet here many families of opulence, and especially ladies, passed several months in the summer, were anxious to get here, and always sorry when the time came to go away.

Buckingham was puzzled by the desire of so many women to assemble at such places; he concluded that "they had been married too early and were bored," and thus any change was pleasant to them.[16] One suspects that in the nineteenth century, when no form of birth control was practiced and children normally came regularly so long as a married woman was of childbearing age, wives were happy to visit the resorts for the few months this kept them away from their husbands.

For social and perhaps for other reasons, the springs in the Shenandoah Valley were the best known in the South and the most popular. Undoubtedly one reason for this popularity was that at these fashionable places one was most likely to meet, if he was of the upper classes, peers from the rest of the country. At Red Sulphur Springs, Buckingham met friends from New York City,

Albany, New Orleans, Philadelphia, Savannah, Charleston, and Baltimore. These people had not come together to enjoy luxurious quarters. The resort had cost $100,000 to erect, and the main building had two stories. Long wings of one-room cabins extended off to each side, one for bachelors, the other for families. "As to washstands, drawers, dressing tables, bed-carpets, or such refinements as these, they were not to be found." [17]

There were many resort springs in Virginia, but White Sulphur Springs, where Washington had bathed in his day, and to which Robert E. Lee would lend his presence after the Civil War, was the most famous and the most fashionable. One year, probably 1840, fifty people were reported at Grey Sulphur Springs; the place was owned by a Mr. Legare, and the guests were mainly South Carolinians. At Red Sulphur Springs there were some two hundred guests, but at White Sulphur between seven hundred and eight hundred. It appeared to Buckingham that guests at this resort "were willing to put up with anything offered them; and the fear of being turned away from the establishment altogether sealed all lips against public fault-finding; though in private and among each other, complaints were reciprocally breathed and interchanged." Furthermore, he said, the food was far from the best. "The fare at the table was thought worse than at any of the other springs, and the servants, almost all negroes, were both dirty and ill-disciplined. The only beds we could procure were mattresses stuffed with straw, and these hard and uneven." [18] John Milton Mackie complained that at the height of the season "there is no such thing as dining satisfactorily at the [White Sulphur] Springs." The dining room was always out of everything. "The scene presents a most ludicrous struggle for bones and cold potatoes." He added that the Frenchman who dined on his moustache was better off than a guest paying two dollars a day. [19]

If White Sulphur Springs earned little praise, other spas nearby did much better. Buckingham found appointments better at Virginia Springs than at Saratoga, and the table well supplied with game, poultry, mutton, milk, and butter. George P. R. James found the buildings at Fauquier Springs excellent and comfortable. Also the place had excellent cooks, and the mutton he believed to be the best in Virginia. At Hot Springs, the Reverend and Mrs. Charles C. Jones, seeking unsuccessfully to restore his health, found "everything . . . bountiful and delightfully prepared: beef, mutton, ham, venison, the best bread, butter, and milk. Our pastry is superior: straw and gooseberry pies, puddings, and plenty of strawberries gathered in the mountains. They are small but finely flavored."[20]

It is impossible to say when the word *hotel* was first used in the Old South, but it was fairly late. In general the word referred to a place in a city or town of some consequence that provided both food and lodging, but by the time of the Civil War many establishments that would have been inns or taverns in an earlier age were calling themselves hotels. Likewise, the term was used at a number of resorts. In general the traveler who sought food and shelter at a hotel fared better than if he were at a country inn or at the home of a family that "took in" travelers, but he could still fall on hard times.

Travelers seem to have been as outraged at their treatment in central Georgia hotels as at the inns and taverns. The Curraghee Hotel near Athens was said to be characterized by "the most miserable fare, filthy servants, and only two enclosed rooms in the house for sleeping." Buckingham used two pages of his book to describe the horrors of his hotel at Columbus. Olmsted also slept at Columbus, or tried to, and found the hotel the worst place he had seen since leaving the District of Columbia. It was "disgustingly dirty; the table revolting; the waiters stupid and inattentive." Olmsted also found food at a "first class" hotel in Memphis "repulsive." This establishment had a menu that listed oyster soup, redfish, nine roasts, nine boiled meats, seventeen entrees, twenty-two vegetables, and twenty desserts. The vegetables included no fewer than six cabbage dishes and two turnip dishes, one of the latter being turnips with drawn butter. Among the boiled meats was "jole and greens," bacon and turnips, codfish-egg sauce, and barbecued rabbits. The entrees included such delicacies as calves' feet in mushroom sauce, calves' feet with Madeira sauce, baked beef kidney, calves' heads with wine, bear sausage, and "harricane tripe," whatever that may have been. Natchez also had some villainous hotels, twelve of them in fact, which made Buckingham marvel again at how unquestioningly and without complaint American travelers accepted bad accommodations and worse food.[21]

Most of the better hotels were found in the larger cities, though there were some fine places in smaller towns. Willard's Hotel in Washington was probably the most famous in the nation. The beginning of the Civil War had no doubt increased the number of its customers, but in 1861 "not less than twenty-five hundred people dine in the public room every day. . . . The servants never cease shoving the chairs to and fro, with a harsh screeching noise over the floor, so that one can hardly hear his neighbor speak. If he did, he would probably hear, as I did at this very hotel, a man order breakfast, 'Black tea and toast, scrambled eggs, fresh spring shad, wild pigeon, pigs' feet, two robins on toast, oysters." Harriet Martineau was in Washington in the fall and was impressed by the presence of so many wild ducks, canvasbacks and otherwise, on the table. Baltimore offered good accommodations, as did Charleston, which after the war restored its hotels before almost anything else. One antebellum traveler noted, however, that the ladies of Charleston had the very common problem of caring for skirts on public floors almost covered with spittle from tobacco chewers.[22]

Harriet Martineau spent a miserable night on a train, but at a hotel in Montgomery, Alabama, she found a breakfast to atone for all. "Besides the tea and coffee, there were corn-bread, beans, buckwheat cakes, broiled chicken, bacon, eggs, rice, hominy, fish, fresh and pickled, and beefsteak." More than a few travelers spoke of good food and accommodations at Montgomery hotels. One tale has it that Montgomery was chosen over Wetumpka as capital of the state because a new hotel passed out copies of its menu among legislators. In Mobile there were reportedly three hostelries as good as any in the North, though the Englishman who conceded this also pointed out that they charged more than northern hotels.[23]

When in New Orleans, Buckingham stayed at the Saint Charles Hotel, which he labeled the "largest and handsomest hotel in the world." There were nearly five hundred guests at the time; three hundred dined at the table set aside for men, some two hundred at the ladies' table. He had high praise for the Saint Louis and Veranda hotels also, but he noted that the cost was double what it would have been in the North.[24] One might well assume that the food at New Orleans hotels was better than that found elsewhere, but little testimony to this effect is to be found. Perhaps Creole fare was too exotic to please the palates of Englishmen, northerners, and people from the upper South who had not had time to learn to appreciate it. Those who lived in the city or nearby knew that their food was superior and therefore felt no need to comment.

Hotels in unlikely places earned praise from time to time, including even the Lanier House at Macon, Georgia, which was described as "very good for the place." Charles C. Jones, Jr., was delighted with the resort hotel at Mammoth Cave, which had "a table well furnished with young chickens, corn bread, and fresh butter for those who may have lingered long in the cave." William Howard Russell, though he formed no high opinion of the clientele, found a hotel at Vicksburg with abundant fare.

> At the end of the room there was a long table on which the joints and dishes were brought hot from the kitchen to be carved by the negro waiters, male and female, and as each was brought in the proprietor, standing in the center of the room, shouted out with a loud voice, "now, then, here is a splendid goose! Ladies and gentlemen, don't neglect the goose and applesauce! Now here's a piece of beef that I can recommend! Upon my honor you will never regret taking a slice of the beef. Oyster pie! Oyster pie! Never was better oyster pie seen in Vicksburg. Run about, boys, and take orders. Ladies and gentlemen, just look at that turkey! Who's for turkey?"—and so on, wiping the perspiration from his forehead and combating with the flies.[25]

Olmsted found an excellent little hotel in Natchitoches, Louisiana. He observed that at the bar more wines than whiskey were sold, and he was impressed by the fact that claret and sauterne were placed on the table for the free use of diners. Texans, he observed, seldom took advantage of this opportunity but instead bought whiskey at the bar. Olmsted noted that light wines were drunk much more extensively in Louisiana than anywhere else in the United States, to such an extent, indeed, that among the Creoles and more prosperous Americans claret was the common breakfast drink.[26]

Hotels in the South operated, of course, on the "American plan," which meant that meals went with the lodgings. Most of them had one common table, though some had several, and some segregated men and women. We know little about the table manners of people in the privacy of their homes. One tends to assume that the elegance attributed to plantation life in general extended to the dining table. But when travelers came together at a hotel the men, at least, behaved more like animals than like gentlemen. Mrs. Trollope watched in horror as fifty diners in a Memphis hotel ran to the table and swallowed potatoes, meat, and bread apparently without chewing. Not a word was spoken; she heard only the sounds of smacking, chomping, and an "unceasing chorus of coughing." James E. Alexander "watched scores of men rush into hotels and boarding houses" in Nashville when the dinner bell sounded, "spitting chewing tobacco in one direction and blowing their noses in the other, to devour chunks of roast beef and loaves of bread like party sandwiches." Henry Ruffner gave perhaps the best description.

> Near meal time you observe the company increase; young men and middle aged men come in . . . they become restless. . . . Wait a little and you will see them simultaneously rush through the door and hurry into the dining room. . . . Before you have time to enter the dining room, you have a thundering of chairs, succeeded instantly by a sharp, confused clatter of plates, dishes, knives, and forks. When you enter the room, you find all the most convenient seats at the table, occupied by a set of men, with heads down and mouths open; and pieces rapidly disappearing from their plates by the quick three-fold operation of a cut—a gape—and a swallow. . . . By the

time you are fairly underway with your meal, you again hear the frequent grating of chairs on the floor as they rise and depart.[27]

Most of the best and most critical descriptions of commercial lodgings in the South are from the pens of northerners and foreigners. Southerners, too, could be highly critical, but they were able to evaluate more realistically. People who disliked southern cooking in general, and especially those who disliked pork, were not likely to find many meals to please them in southern establishments. Nor was the service likely to please them; southerners put up with a great deal of slovenliness in the service in their own homes. Slaves who worked as menials in a hotel or tavern were even less likely to endeavor to please. They quickly learned, moreover, to give especially poor service to the customer who neglected to tip them. But it was not all bad. One anonymous Englishman, after detailing many miseries of southern travel, wrote that his party was quite likely "to be reconciled at last to all our miseries, and quite sorry that the journey is over, because we have performed the last half of it with some really charming family, and have laughed in company at what we groaned at alone."[28]

The old ways were on their way out. In 1866 Mrs. Charles C. Jones ate breakfast at the Saint Cloud Hotel in Nashville, "which is served entirely by white servants; and everything was clean and nice and arranged in the eating line after the present approved style of separate tables and ordering whatever you wish, which comes up hot and in a variety of small dishes." But all the old ways were not completely gone. The famous De Soto Hotel in Savannah gave its guests a free Christmas dinner in 1891. The centerpiece "represented a team of suckling pigs harnessed to a wagon driven by Santa Claus, and loaded with boned turkey garnished with quail. . . . The second piece was an immense salmon, decorated in green, red, and black and lying upon a bed of green moss made of frozen suet and butter. At the head of the table sat two wild turkeys with their wings and feathers "on as alive," and at the foot there rested two proud hams, one figured in sugar representing a vase of flowers, and the other checkered like a chess board."[29]

6

Cornmeal and Salt Pork

THE FOOD OF THE SLAVES

What a slave ate in the Old South depended largely on when and where he lived. On the frontier he usually ate whatever his owner ate, though one suspects that he got the less desirable portions of the game, fish, or domestic animals consumed. Later, if he was one of the few bondsmen belonging to a yeoman farmer family, his food again was likely to be the same as the whites, though he probably did not get wheaten bread or sweets on the rare occasions when his master had them. On a plantation the allowance of food was likely to be more uniform, and the average plantation slave probably had a more adequate diet than his peer on a small farm. Slaves in town had almost exactly the same food as their owners unless they were hired out and allowed to feed themselves. In either case, their problem was not so much quality as quantity. The evidence is fairly conclusive that slave food improved as the years passed; they certainly got a greater quantity of food, and almost certainly their diet contained a greater proportion of protein.[1]

The slave's bread was corn bread. If separate rations were issued to each family, the allowance was usually a peck of cornmeal per week for each adult, something less for the children. In the eighteenth and early nineteenth centuries, the corn was often issued in the ear and thus had to be shelled and ground or pounded into meal, but this burden on already hard-worked slaves became much less common with the passage of time. Whether the bread was made in the family's cabin or in a communal plantation kitchen, almost always the meal was mixed with water and baked in the fireplace ashes with no shortening. The batter was often cooked on the blade of a hoe, hence the term hoecake. Flour was seldom issued to blacks. On the Tidewater rice plantations rice cake often replaced corn bread, and in some areas sweet potatoes were substituted for corn bread at least part of the time. One former slave remembered:

> Us slaves was fed good plain grub. Before we went to de field us had a big breakfast o' hot bread, 'lasses, fried salt meat dipped in cornmeal, and fried taters. Sometimes us had fish and rabbit meat. When us was in the field, two women would come at dinner time with baskets filled with corn pone, baked taters, corn roasted in de shucks, onion, fried squash, and . . . at supper time us had hoecakes and cold victuals. Sometimes dey was sweet milk and collards.
>
> Most every slave had his own little garden patch. . . . Most every plantation kept a man huntin' and fishin' all the time. . . . On Sundays us always had meat pie or fish or fresh game and roasted taters and coffee. On Christmas de marster would give us chicken and barrels o'apples and oranges. 'Course, every marster weren't as free handed as ours was.[2]

Pork was as much the staple meat for black southerners as for white. On small farms, and on plantations where much of the pork was purchased, slaves could expect the less desirable cuts, few hams and much fatback. On the large plantations where scores or perhaps hundreds of hogs were slaughtered, there was no way the planter and his family could eat all the best pieces, and many of them found their way to the slave quarter. At hog killing time on farm or plantation, blacks and whites participated in an orgy of eating fresh pork; otherwise much of it would have spoiled. The evidence is conclusive that black southerners preferred pork to other kinds of meat. Those whose masters, fleeing before Union troops, took them to Texas during the Civil War, made their way back east complaining that in Texas they got too much beef and too little pork. Whether for lack of utensils, lack of time, or taste preference, blacks tended even more than whites to boil their pork.[3]

Obviously, those who lived in the slave quarter did get other kinds of meat from time to time. Beef was distributed fairly frequently during the late summer and fall when the supply of cured pork was exhausted or nearing exhaustion. Beef was considered to be much less nutritious than pork, however. The pork ration on most plantations was from two and one-half to three and one-half pounds per adult per week; the beef ration was often two pounds per day. Here and there, especially near the Atlantic, some masters gave out mutton with some regularity, and those on the coast or on a tidal stream might make fish a major item in the slave diet. A beef, a kid, a sheep, more often a hog, sometimes several or all of these, were barbecued for special occasions, especially for Christmas and the Fourth of July.[4]

Many slaves were permitted to keep chickens and presumably from time to time they ate their birds, but one gets the impression that most of the fryers were sold to the master. Cockerels, of course, had a much lower life expectancy than pullets, and a laying hen was much too valuable to kill. It is impossible to determine to what extent slaves ate eggs, but most eggs too were probably sold to the master, a neighbor, or in a nearby town.

Slaves could, of course, devour chickens that they had not reared. They stole them, and ducks and geese and turkeys too, from their masters, from neighbors, and to some degree from one another. For that matter, many cows and hogs fell victim to the blacks' hunger, or perhaps, to their simple desire for a change in diet. It seems obvious that black people understood the injustice of slavery well enough to feel little guilt when appropriating white property. A planter whose animals were stolen and eaten by his own bondsmen could ruefully comfort himself with the thought that his people were better nourished as a result, but when a neighbor's slaves raided his flocks and herds, he complained mightily. If the slave narratives recorded during the 1930s can be believed, many blacks took pride in their skill at making away with chickens, pigs, cattle, and even cured pork from the smokehouse. Some of them, in their old age, insisted that stolen meat was better, and this was perhaps literally true. It was nonetheless a wasteful practice, because too often some of the meat was left to rot in the woods.[5]

The presence of a black hunter on a plantation did not necessarily mean that the slaves ate game; the venison and other meat
the hunter provided almost always went to the big house, not to
the quarter. Slaves who consumed game were more likely to eat
rabbit, which could be caught in simple snares and traps, or the
nocturnal coon or possum. Solomon Northup, who for twelve years
labored as a slave in Louisiana, said that coon was good, but that
"nothing in all butcherdom [was] so delicious as roasted possum."[6]
The fondness of blacks for possum has no doubt been exaggerated, but it did exist, and for good reason. At night, when the creature was abroad, the slave was not working; moreover, this marsupial was a slow traveler who could be chased up a tree by any
dog that had learned to trail possums and let rabbits alone. It was
not essential, hardly even desirable, that the dog bark on the trail;
all that was necessary was that he bark treed. For hunting coon a
bigger and faster dog with a keener nose, preferably a hound, was
needed. Also, a coon was more likely to climb a tree too large to cut
and too difficult to climb. The possum usually went up a small
tree; when he chose a large one he was likely to take refuge on one
of the lower limbs. It was easy to shake him out, and when he hit
the ground he usually pretended to be dead. The hunter merely
picked him up by the tail and dropped him into a sack. Finally, a
healthy possum is one of the fattest animals in the world; roasted
with sweet potatoes he provided calories that no doubt were needed.

Slaves also ate fish when they could. This was obviously true of
those whose masters made fish a part of the rations, but many
blacks caught fish for themselves. Some were taken on hook and
line, thus providing recreation as well as food, but in the interior
most fish seem to have been taken in traps or baskets. The ability
to make a good fish trap was a prized skill among black people well
into the twentieth century. Slaves, like their masters, preferred
catfish; even a stew made from catfish heads was relished. But
they ate almost any fish obtainable; they were happy to get even
bowfin and garfish, species not eaten by whites except in south
Louisiana. Slaves in the interior were so fond of fish that one wonders if their rations did not lack some element that fish provided.[7]

Except for milk, antebellum southern blacks had very few dairy products in their diet. Probably most of them never saw cheese, nor was butter much more common. Indeed, they received whole milk only when enough cows were fresh to provide it; most of the time, if they got any milk at all, it was buttermilk. Buttermilk was, incidentally, a very important item in the diet of slave children. Slave families were rarely given a cow and made responsible for the production of their own milk. Perhaps, after their stint in the fields, they did not have time and energy to milk a cow and take proper care of the milk. Probably, too, the black family did not have, and the master was not willing to provide, the utensils needed for handling milk.[8]

Whether they lived on a plantation or a small farm, most slaves had an adequate supply of vegetables. Their owners usually knew that vegetables were an essential part of a balanced diet, and plant foods produced on the land were much cheaper than pork, beef, or mutton. Slaves ate the same leafy vegetables as whites, turnip greens, often with turnips, ranking first in importance. Cabbage was a favorite of both races, but the rather strong-flavored collard was better liked by blacks than by most whites. Hominy, grits, and green corn in season were available to black and white; beans were not so frequent a fare outside of southern Louisiana, but they were far from unknown. Cowpeas, as could be anticipated, were a major item in the slave's nourishment; available all year either green or dry, they could even substitute for meat. Sweet potatoes were just as important if not more so. Where it was grown, rice was a common cereal, often covered with peas, beans, or some spicy Creole mixture. East of the Mississippi, "hoppin' John" was a fairly common slave dish. The ingredients apparently varied; in Alabama it was primarily grits and peas; in South Carolina rice was mixed with the peas.[9]

There is little evidence that slave families cooked or in any way prepared fruit in their cabins, but sometimes fruits were cooked for them in communal kitchens. They certainly ate fruit raw on those plantations that had orchards, and they ate wild fruits everywhere. No doubt more fruit would have been eaten, and to the benefit of all concerned, had it not been that many people believed that the eating of fresh fruit was unhealthful.[10]

Seemingly children, and this was certainly true of those on plantations, did not eat as well as adults who were able to work in the fields. When a slave family prepared its own food, the children presumably ate what their parents ate, though almost surely not as much, and probably not proportionately as much meat. They may have received more whole milk and buttermilk than their parents. On plantations where children were fed from a communal kitchen, it was a common practice for them to eat a mixture of milk or buttermilk and corn bread from a trough. One former slave described his childhood eating.

> Dere was a great long trough that went plum across de yard, and dat was where us [children] et. For dinner we had peas or some other sort of vegetable, and corn bread. Aunt Viney crumbled up that bread in that trough and poured the vegetables and pot likker over it. Den she blowed de horn and chillen come a-runnin from every which way. If us et it all up, she had to put more victuals in de trough and poured buttermilk over it. We never had nothin' but corn bread and buttermilk at night. Sometimes dat trough would be a sight, 'cause we never stopped to wash our hands, and before us had been eatin' more dan a minute or two what was in de trough would look like real mud what had come off our hands.[11]

Molasses and corn bread was a special treat for slave children. Two generations after the Civil War corn bread and molasses, carried in a gallon pail, was sometimes the lunch brought to school by poor children, black and white. Many masters also gave a ration of molasses, or perhaps sorghum syrup, to their adult slaves. Apparently the slave children received an adequate diet; there is little or no evidence of widespread malnutrition among the slave children of the southern United States, though there were certainly scattered instances.[12]

The preparation of the slave's food was necessarily simple. It has been suggested that slaves cooked in African style to the extent that they could and, indeed, that so-called southern cooking is an adaptation of the African cuisine.[13] This assumption is almost certainly incorrect. The best available book on African cooking, which devotes much attention to western Africa, supports no such inference. Indeed, the emphasis on pepper and other spices that characterizes southern cooking in itself refutes the idea of African origins, because all peppers except black pepper and many other spices originated in the New World and were carried from there to Africa.[14] It is a fact, however, that the "soul food" in vogue among urban blacks in the late 1960s was more or less the food that southern blacks ate as slaves. But it was also practically the same food that yeoman farmers and poor whites ate; it was derived from England, the Indians, and the frontier experience far more than from Africa.

Hoecake, sweet potatoes, and green corn could be and were cooked in the coals of the slave cabin's mud-and-stick fireplace, and fresh meat was sometimes roasted over the coals on an improvised spit. Certainly stolen animals were cooked over open fires in the woods. Most of the time, however, slave food was either boiled or fried, and boiling was more common than frying. This was as much a matter of necessity as of choice. Often one pot was the only cooking utensil available; what could not be cooked in the coals had to be tossed into the pot. Nor was this a great hardship; this was how the pioneer family had cooked in the early years of settlement. Many white families continued to rely primarily on the stewpot for long years after the frontier had passed. The cooking pot was often the serving dish as well, the entire family eating from it with wooden spoons. Some planters, on the other hand, not only provided plates for the cabins but even sent them to the fields for the noon meal. The cooking of meat and vegetables together in the same pot was only a variation from the white practice of boiling vegetables with a piece of fat salt pork added for flavor. Since people come to like what they eat, and since the basic diet of southern blacks probably changed only for the worse in the years following the Civil War, black people continued to boil much of their food into the twentieth century and, to some extent, until today.[15]

In addition to whole milk and buttermilk, many indulgent masters provided coffee from time to time, and slaves who were allowed to earn money might buy it. Blacks also prepared coffee substitutes from cowpeas, sweet potatoes, and other things, just as some whites did. Obviously, however, the main drink of the slave was water, and in the fields on hot days great quantities were needed. A source of good water was essential to plantation or homestead. This water might come from dug wells, and it could come from a particularly copious spring, but as often as not it came from a nearby stream. Whatever the perils to health, such water was usually good to the taste; in my youth, water from the Mississippi River, which did not yet contain such pollutants as gasoline and carbolic acid, tasted good, however burdened it may have been with sediment and other matter.

Almost if not entirely everywhere in the Old South it was illegal to give or sell whiskey to slaves. Yet newspapers published many editorials complaining of the nuisance of drunken blacks loafing in towns on Saturday afternoons and Sundays. Masters often gave their hands a drink or two when they had worked unusually hard or in celebration of some special occasion such as a holiday or a wedding. On many sugar plantations a drink was routine for the "night watch" during the grinding season. But even if their masters believed in total abstinence for all the world, black people were resourceful enough to acquire a jug from time to time. Many of them did earn some money, and almost always they could find some entrepreneur to supply their needs. Some slaves were not above stealing a ham or some other easily negotiable property from the smokehouse and trading it for liquor. This infuriated slave owners. Not only was the property lost, but a drunken slave might become a disciplinary problem. If he drank enough, his capacity for effective work the next day was definitely reduced.

In general the diet of adult slaves, like that of their children, seems to have been adequate. Slaves did suffer from intestinal parasites of various repulsive types, but so did whites. The diet almost certainly sufficed in calories; estimates range from four thousand to five thousand calories per day, enough to sustain much hard labor. This hard labor, incidentally, seems to have been sufficient to prevent the high incidence of coronary heart disease that might otherwise have been expected from a diet containing so much fat pork. Or it may have been that the state of medicine in the nine-teenth century, certainly dismal, was so bad that other diseases took off most slaves before they had time to develop heart trouble. Definite cases of malnutrition among slaves are hard to identify, but there was almost certainly an outbreak of beriberi on planta-tions near New Orleans from 1818 into the 1820s. Recent investiga-tions also show that there may have been an outbreak of pellagra, that scourge of the New South, in the hard years following the Panic of 1837.[16]

There were exceptions, but most of the surviving former slaves interviewed during the 1930s seem to have had fond memories of the food they had eaten as bondsmen. One recalled that "we had plenty to eat, like meat and bread and vegetables." Another as-serted: "Master Joe was a good provider, and we always had plenty of corn pone, sow belly and greens, sweet potatoes, cow peas, and cane molasses. . . . Sometimes coffee, too." A third remembered: "In those days we had plenty of good plain food, such as pot likker, greens, cornbread, taters, peas, pears, and at hog killin' us had chittlins and pig jowls and back bone. . . . Us never seed no flour, though." Finally, "Good gracious, what we had to eat. They gave us plenty—turnip greens and hog jowl and peas and corn bread, and milk by the barrels."[17]

Perhaps this approbation of the slave diet by former slaves came about because black people in general were so abysmally poor from the time of emancipation to World War II. I, for one, am con-vinced that on the average the slaves of the Old South had more and better food to eat than the sharecroppers, black and white, of the post-Civil War era. But another fact to be remembered is that those former slaves still alive in the 1930s were very old men and women. Their memories in the 1930s may well have been more abundant and tasty than the food they actually ate in the 1850s.

7

Long Years and Short Rations

THE CIVIL WAR

As most southerners went joyously into the Civil War, few gave thought to the problems involved in feeding the new nation and its armies. Yet these problems deserved much attention, because in some respects the South had not been self-sufficient in food when at peace. Pork was the chief meat in the diet of nearly everyone except perhaps the richer planters, and the Deep South imported large quantities of pork from the North each year. The South did produce many swine, but the quality was low; and what was true of hogs was even more true of the South's tough little range cattle.

It has often been asserted that the Confederacy had an abundance of food, but that an imperfect and continuously worsening distribution system kept the Rebel armies hungry. Certainly southern communications were primitive by modern standards, and they did worsen rapidly as the war went on. Also, the Confederate government's administration of its armies' rations could hardly have been more inefficient. Probably, also, the South's production of foodstuffs, especially meat, declined as the war went on. The greatest decline was east of the Mississippi River, and after the fall of Vicksburg and Port Hudson it made little or no difference to the main Confederate armies how many longhorn cattle there were in Texas or how many razorback hogs rooted in north Louisiana and Arkansas. No statistical studies have been done on the subject, and it is doubtful that enough firm figures could be produced to make such a study meaningful; but it can certainly be argued that the South simply did not produce enough food to support itself in a long war.[1]

Whatever the foodstuffs produced in 1860, the amount available was reduced sharply once the fighting had begun. Probably more than three quarters of a million of the strongest men in the Confederacy saw military service, and most of them came from farms and plantations. The loss of this much labor inevitably reduced agricultural production. Small farms suffered most severely; planters could plant less cotton and more food crops, though many did continue to plant cotton. But even those who did their best to produce food for the Confederacy found that circumstances limited what they could do. It certainly did not help the Rebel armies for a planter in middle or western Tennessee or in the sugar parishes of Louisiana to plant more corn, potatoes, and peas after those regions were occupied by the Union. Many blacks were conscripted by Confederate officials for labor details; tens of thousands were enlisted in the Union army; and scores of thousands, most of them the youngest and strongest adults, flocked to the Federal forces as they came near. The soldiers on both sides not only emptied the smokehouses and corncribs; they ate the animals that had been kept for later slaughtering and for breeding. More than that, they carried away the horses and mules that were essential to the cultivation of any crops, whether foodstuffs or staples. By the end of the struggle many planters were content if they could produce enough corn to feed themselves and the blacks who remained on the plantation; small farmers were often hungry.[2]

But in the beginning food was not a problem. William Howard Russell, though he voiced the European's usual distaste for overcooking and for the excess of pork on southern tables, found abundant victuals as he traveled through the South in 1861. At Mobile he noted full fruit and vegetable stands, and he was especially impressed by "oyster saloons," where he ate oysters in a pudding, fried, roasted, in a stew, broiled, and raw. In one of the forts guarding the harbor he ate with the officers and enjoyed fish, fried ham, fried onions, biscuits, coffee, and good wine. Obviously ordinary people did not eat this well, but even in 1862 the war seems to have had relatively little effect upon the food that graced people's tables. Even such imported items as coffee did not become too scarce, because the northern blockade did not become at all effective until about mid-1862, and it was not nearly so stringent then as it would be later.[3]

By 1863 the effects of war in general and the blockade in particular were felt much more severely, and the most galling shortage was of salt. Southerners had enough salt to season their food, but they did not have enough to cure pork. Before the end of 1862 a Mississippi planter wrote: "We have corn for bread; we have hogs for meat, but no salt to save it."[4] Before the war most of the salt used in the South had been imported from England, but once the blockade was established, armaments and luxuries brought the blockade runners much higher profits. The Confederacy did make the most of the salt it had. The almost limitless deposits on Avery Island in Louisiana were exploited until the works were destroyed by Union action. Salt springs and salt licks scattered over the Confederacy were used to the greatest extent possible with the techniques of the times. Those who lived near the sea boiled salt from salt water. Farmers even dug up the dirt under their smokehouses, put it in water, and then boiled it down to recover the salt that had collected over the years. But all this produced only a drop in the bucket as compared to the need. The shortage of salt was so critical and made such an impression that it was one of the most vivid memories of those children who remained at home during the war and who lived to tell me tales of their childhood.[5]

Whether the Confederacy ever had enough swine to feed its people and its armies is debatable. In such a debate it would be necessary to remember that hogs behind the Union lines in Virginia, Tennessee, or elsewhere were of no use to Rebel soldiers except during the rare invasions of Union and Union-occupied territory. How many pigs there were in the woods hardly matters anyway; it is certain that from early 1863 on, there was not enough cured pork to meet the demand. No doubt there was a significant increase in the amount of fresh pork eaten by civilians, white and slave, but soldiers could not put live hogs, or even fresh pork chops, in their knapsacks as provisions for a three-day march. Since salt bacon could no longer be had from Cincinnati or other places in the Northwest, and because the scarcity of salt prevented its being produced at home, some of the precious space aboard blockade runners was used for barrels of pickled pork. It must have been pretty bad; as hungry as Confederate soldiers usually were, they called this stuff "nauseous bacon." Beef played a much larger role than pork in the rations of the average southern soldier.[6]

At least some pork remained; sugar almost disappeared completely. The fall of New Orleans cut off the supply from Louisiana, but even in peacetime Louisiana had produced only brown sugar; white sugar had come from the North or abroad. At the same time the supply of sugar was cut off, so was the supply of cane molasses. Except for a fortunate few who had access to honey or to maple syrup, and a very few in Florida who could grow sugarcane, southerners east of the Mississippi River had to depend on sorghum. Sorghum syrup was not as sweet as cane molasses, and it was likely to sour or crystallize, or both, rather quickly. But when it was the only sweetening available, people were happy to have it. Certainly it was better than the syrup a few people attempted to produce from corn stalks or watermelons. Sorghum must have been rather abundant, because it was issued to slaves fairly regularly during the war.[7]

From the contemporary accounts, one would assume that the greatest hardship of the Civil War South was the scarcity or complete absence of coffee. Probably some class bias is involved here, because upper-class people kept most of the records, and many lower-class people had made do with substitutes for years before 1861. Once the blockade had become effective, almost everything imaginable was tried as a substitute. Among the substances poured into coffee cups were parched rye, wheat, corn, peanuts, persimmon seed, and watermelon seed. According to one source, mature and carefully browned okra seed were closest in flavor to real coffee; next in preference were sweet potatoes cut into small pieces, dried, then parched. If one may judge from the satisfaction with which the fortunate drank a cup of real coffee, none of these sub-

stitutes was really satisfactory. Troops in contact with the enemy
were sometimes able to barter for coffee during periods of no fighting, but this was seldom possible for civilians in Confederate-con-
trolled territory.[8]

Ingenious housewives and soldiers devised substitutes for many
other once-standard items of food and drink. Tea was made from
sassafras roots, as it had been before the war and would be after,
but sage leaves, holly leaves, blackberry leaves, and in Florida
orange leaves were also dried and boiled as tea. Roasted and
pounded peanuts were said to be a good substitute for chocolate,
and "lemonade" was made from maypops and pomegranates. As
for condiments, mustard was made from mustard seed, and red
pepper, necessarily used with care and moderation, was an adequate substitute for black pepper. Good vinegar was made from
honey and from apple cider, and a barely usable vinegar from persimmons. As had been done for generations, thirsty souls made
beer from persimmons, and some also tried home brew made from
corn, potatoes, and sassafras. Some observant, experimental-
minded housewives learned that if corncob ashes were allowed to
stand in water until the water cleared, the resultant solution
mixed with two parts of sour milk was a substitute for baking
powder.[9] Since baking powder had been manufactured commercially only since about 1850, its absence was not a great hardship.

Obviously people in the towns were sooner and more seriously
affected by shortages than people on the land; this was true
whether the shortage resulted from maldistribution in the midst of
plenty or from inadequate production. Even when town dwellers
had a garden, which most of them did, vegetables fended off hunger for only part of the year. Poultry and pigs helped, but the pork
normally could not be preserved, and chickens were especially
likely to become the prey of marauding troops of both armies. A
milch cow was figuratively worth her weight in gold, and toward
the end she might have literally been worth her weight in Confederate currency, but she could not give milk constantly, and
cows were too often the victims of foragers or simple thieves. The
constant inflation of Confederate currency put town people who

lived on wages at a special disadvantage, because prices constantly outpaced wages; when farm products were on the market,
workers in the towns often could not buy. Inflation was especially
damaging to the wives and children of men in the army. Even
when the soldiers were paid, and often they were not, and even if
they were able to send their pay home, it was not nearly enough by
itself to support a wife and children. Some states paid small al-
lowances to soldiers' wives (or widows), but this was little in the
beginning and completely inadequate after inflation had begun.[10]

The fact that hunger led to widespread rioting in 1863 is an
often ignored part of Civil War history. At least thirteen food riots
occurred, the most important ones in Salisbury and Bladensboro,
North Carolina, Mobile and Richmond. Since men were away at
war, the rioters were principally women. They were from the lower
levels of white society, they had no organization, and they themselves probably felt ashamed of such unfeminine self-assertion.
Yet there was true desperation in the statement of a young woman
in Richmond: "We celebrate our right to live. We are starving. As
soon as enough of us get together we are going to the bakeries and
each of us will take a loaf of bread. This is little enough for the
government to give us after it has taken our men."[11] Certainly
these women were castigated by better-fed officials and official
families for the harm they did the Confederate cause. Need, so it
was said, was not the real cause of such unladylike behavior,
though no critics were able to identify the "real cause." In truth,
the rioters were in the main hungry women with hungry children
to feed. After 1863 there was no improvement in supply or distribution, but apparently there were no more riots until the fall of
Richmond. Perhaps hunger had left lower-class townswomen too
apathetic to assert themselves.[12]

In general, conditions in the country were better than in town,
but that depended on where one was in the country. The already
poverty-stricken areas of Appalachia and the Ozarks were devastated by conflicts between local Unionists and Secessionists even
before the campaigns of 1863 brought additional hardship. Plantation whites usually fared better; we read of a planter's wife who

sent much-appreciated Christmas gifts of ordinary food items to her friends and relatives in town. But even in the more fertile regions, the passage of a foraging army could leave much suffering in its wake. By 1863 the misery of Confederate civilians was very real. The fortunate had a barely adequate diet of peas, corn bread, and bacon; the unfortunate had much less. An English officer passing through Alabama in 1863 noted that the women whose husbands were in service were dressed in rags and that they had only the coarsest food to eat. In North Carolina more than five hundred women petitioned the governor for relief, warning that many would starve if something was not done for them. One woman who had five sons in the army wrote that she and her other children had had no bread for three days and that they had no prospect for food in the future. Mrs. Roger Pryor, wife of a Confederate general, almost starved in December of 1862 at Petersburg, waiting to give birth to a child. Many of the poor people who lacked food might have been on short rations, though certainly not approaching starvation, had there been no war. But the war took away the men, and the women and small children could not do all the heavy work necessary to make a normal corn crop, even if they were fortunate enough to have and keep a horse, mule, or ox to draw the plow. For that matter, with no men about, it was difficult even for a family to supply itself with wood for cooking. Certainly few women and children could catch and slaughter range hogs, even if they had salt to cure the meat.[13]

No definitive study has been made of the effect of the Civil War upon slave diet. The scarcity of cured pork could be compensated for, at least in part, by passing out more fresh meat and by increasing the amount of beans and cowpeas in the rations. Generally, however, as the war went on the slaves got more corn and sweet potatoes and less meat. Plantation records show that the slaves responded by doing less work and by increasing their forays against cattle and hogs that were within their reach after the sun had gone down. No doubt, also, possums, coons, rabbits, and fish lived more hazardous lives than before. It would be interesting to know how much the quite definite "slowdown" in slave work came from dissatisfaction and how much it came from fewer calories. Anyone who has observed ill-fed Asiatic laborers at work can appreciate how much difference diet can make. Also, one wonders to what extent unsatisfactory plantation rations inspired the tens of thousands of blacks who followed the Union armies as they marched through the South. The admittedly bad rations of the contraband camps may have been better than wartime rations on the plantations.[14]

Yet it was generally agreed during the war that slaves received more adequate food than Confederate soldiers. As early as the Fort Donelson campaign of the winter of 1862 a shortage of rations affected Rebel military decisions. During the Peninsular campaign of the same year many units made do for days without any regular, and very little irregular, food supply. It may be that the almost unbelievably incompetent Confederate commissary never realized that men actively campaigning needed more to eat than men idle in camp; at any rate, it was during periods of marching and fighting that Rebel troops were most hungry. Some of Jubal Early's men in the Shenandoah Valley lived for days on a few ounces of raw bacon; and for a time as General John B. Hood marched out of Alabama toward disaster at Franklin and Nashville, his troops struggled through ankle-deep mud on a ration of two biscuits a day. If General Lee had wanted to evacuate Petersburg earlier, which he considered, he could not have done so, because his men were too weak for hard marches. And when he did withdraw, the hunger of his gaunt army was a major factor in forcing his surrender.[15]

The mainstay of the Confederate soldier was corn bread, but "hardtack" biscuits, which kept well, were issued when they were to be had. The soldier did receive issues of cured bacon—some of it "nauseous"—from time to time, but mainly his meat, when he had any, was fresh beef. Southern beef was not good to begin with, but soldiers believed that the contractors who sold cattle to the army selected the worst animals from a poor lot. The meat, as described by officers and men, was certainly not attractive. It was "sticky and blue," and if a quarter were "thrown against a wall it would stick." The animals driven into camp were so poor and sickly that "it takes two hands to hold up one beef to shoot it." The meat tasted so bad that "buzzards would not eat it at any season of the year." The Rebel soldier was a good forager, and when he could he ate chickens, pigs, and even milch cows, which, as he explained to his officers, he had had to shoot in self-defense. He often ate captured Yankee rations. Now and then he got leafy vegetables, and sweet potatoes and cowpeas were an important part of his diet. Some fortunate men occasionally received food packages from home. But in the main the Confederate soldier fought the war sustained by bad corn bread and worse beef, and even these unattractive foods were too often not to be had.[16]

The hunger that was widespread in the Confederacy in 1863 was much worse in 1864 and 1865. Abandoned fields were too grown up in weeds and brush to be worked, and more fields were abandoned. Contending armies consumed much of the little that was left in Arkansas and Missouri, and Nathaniel Banks's 1864 debacle devastated Louisiana's Red River Valley. But Sherman in Georgia and South Carolina and Sheridan in the Shenandoah Valley did the worst damage. These examples of total war came mostly in the autumn; the raiders made bounteous hauls from cribs and smokehouses full of food set aside for the winter. The people left behind faced hunger, if not starvation, until more food could be planted and harvested. Nor must it be forgotten that Confederate armies, struggling for their very existence, lived off the country directly or indirectly. Of necessity impressment officers took what they could, and in the field, men with rifles in their hands were not going to starve while civilians had full bellies. In Georgia, Wheeler's Confederate cavalry was at least as merciless as Sherman's bummers, and I, who had a great uncle with Forrest, nonetheless heard my elders tell many times how these fierce Confederate fighters stripped corncribs and smokehouses in west Tennessee.

Examples of hunger are endless. As in 1863, the people in town suffered most. In Richmond, simply finding enough to eat was a full-time occupation for many, especially refugees. Families were reduced to one meal a day, and that a sparse one. One woman testified that she had tasted milk only twice in a year; another, of education and breeding, informed a questioner that she had had nothing to eat that day, and that she and her children had existed for three weeks on three pints of rice. Kate Cumming, sprightly daughter of a prominent Mobile family, was thankful for peas, corn meal, and bacon in January of 1865, and in April, as the war was almost at an end, she assured a visitor that she was getting a special meal because the corn bread contained soda, lard, and a whole egg.[17]

Poorer people in the country also suffered. Conditions bad in 1863 were worse in 1864 and tragic in early 1865. How the responsibility for faltering Confederate morale should be apportioned between military defeats and conditions at home is impossible to say, but soldiers did receive piteous letters from their families. One young wife wrote: "Before God, Edward, unless you come home we must die. Last night I was aroused by little Eddie's crying. . . . He said 'Oh Mama, I'm so hungry!' And Lucy, Edward, your darling Lucy, she never complains, but she is growing thinner and thinner every day."[18] Small wonder that so many Confederate soldiers came to see the struggle as "a rich man's war and a poor man's fight" and deserted when the opportunity arose. The real wonder is that so many thousands remained faithful to the very end. Even so, when the war was over, thousands of southern whites had to turn to the hated Freedmen's Bureau for food.

Southerners had always been great drinkers of water, but the war, greatly reducing the supply of other potables, forced even greater dependence upon well, spring, or stream. Imported wines and liqueurs became extremely scarce as the blockade tightened, but blockade runners brought a few cases into Charleston, Mobile, and Wilmington almost to the very end. Probably there was a decline in the amount of whiskey distilled, but this would be hard to prove. Louisiana's Governor Henry Watkins Allen's efforts to prevent corn's being made into whiskey (except in a state-operated "laboratory" that was supposedly making medicine) failed, and Governor Joseph E. Brown of Georgia made similar efforts with no greater success. Probably the requisitioning of copper worms to be made into caps for percussion cap rifles reduced the whiskey supply more than government edicts. Even so, Confederate troops and their officers had fairly frequent access to strong drink. Perhaps there was a decline in quality; the names soldiers gave to what they drank suggest savage hangovers.[19]

Obviously the war put a great strain on southern hospitality. A family that was itself short of food could hardly be expected to look with delight upon the arrival of a refugee relative and her numerous children. In the main, however, relatives were dutifully accepted, with resignation if not with enthusiasm. Especially was this true of the aristocracy, which tended to be related by blood, marriage, or common acquaintance all over the South. But even the relatively poor countrymen seem to have done their best for the "quality" when hard times had come upon them. The daughters of a distinguished South Carolinian, fleeing across their state to avoid Sherman, were received courteously by strangers six nights out of seven. One host had no food, but he gave them a bed and rode with them part way the next morning. The others shared however little or much they had.

Other refugees were not so fortunate. If they fled to a town, as many of them did, they might well encounter hostility rather than hospitality. Sometimes the refugee wife and children of a planter were seen by an undernourished and war-weary people as members of the class that had brought on the war, and their sufferings were looked upon as a deserved punishment. Refugees were also victims of the inexorable depreciation of Confederate currency. Rents were so high that more than a few women and children were forced to take shelter in abandoned and half-ruined slave cabins or in empty railroad cars. The social round of visitation that had prevailed before the war came to an almost complete end, but it would be resumed after the end of hostilities.[20]

The political and economic effects of the Civil War upon the South were great, and the psychological effects were probably greater. Changes in eating habits brought about by the struggle were, however, of short duration. The Confederate veteran who had fought the war on corn bread and beef continued to eat corn bread, but he quickly returned to pork as the main meat in his diet.

The slave was transformed into a sharecropper and came to live more and more on corn bread and pork alone with fewer and fewer fruits and vegetables in his diet. His pork and cornmeal, in fact, were of lower quality than he had eaten as a slave. As the years passed, more and more whites were reduced to sharecropping, and their diet was not significantly different from that of blacks. A very few blacks and more whites prospered to some extent, and their diet was somewhat changed by improvements in transportation and food technology. Even so, the most striking fact about southern food from the end of the Civil War to World War II is how much it resembled the food of the Old South. Changes began, but in the countryside the old ways would remain strong for two generations.

8

Bacon, Biscuits, and Sometimes Ham

THE NEW SOUTH

It is unnecessary to elaborate upon the fact that the Civil War left the South poorer than it had been in antebellum years; the section remained one of the nation's major economic problems into and after the New Deal of the 1930s. Some southerners, black and white, lived in such abject poverty that their inadequate diet and its consequences demand separate treatment in a subsequent chapter. This chapter deals with the food eaten by those who were looked upon by themselves and their neighbors as adequately fed. Some were well-to-do, but most were not. A family of today living as ordinary southerners did then might be considered poverty stricken, but it would have been truly dangerous to have offered charity to such a family in 1880, 1890, or even 1930. Most southerners remained on the land, but the postwar expansion of railroads and the development of general stores led to the growth of existing towns and hamlets and the creation of others. Among ordinary men and women life in town was believed to be in some way superior to life on the farm, though in practice there was not that much difference in the way people lived in small towns and the country. The cities were a different story, but even city people's diet was not so radically different from that of country people.

Technology was largely responsible for the relatively few dietary changes that did come about. The cooking stove had appeared about 1840, but it was uncommon in the South until after the Civil War. Many families cooked in a fireplace for a time after 1865, but by 1900 most kitchens included a stove. The cookstove certainly made life easier for the housewife who did her own cooking, but the kitchen separated from the house, advantageous before the coming of the stove because it kept cooking odors out of the dwelling and reduced the risk of fire, became highly inconvenient. As a result, substantial farmers extended an "el" back to contain the old kitchen, now outfitted with a stove. Baking especially was much easier in a stove than in a brick oven or over coals; a good oven, baking powder, and cheap flour made biscuits a rival of corn bread.

The coming of kerosene also brought change. The kerosene lamp, however fragile the chimney might be, however much it had to be adjusted to get the wick just right, and however dim the light might be in comparison to the fluorescent bulb of a century later, was far superior to candles. Breakfast could be prepared earlier in the morning, and, at least in winter, it became customary to eat supper by lamplight. The faint odor of kerosene never quite left the house. Oil stoves, which sold fairly well for a time, never became truly popular because most foods cooked on them tasted ever so slightly of kerosene. The pervasiveness of the fluid was such that merchants tried to keep their coal oil barrels away from foods; indeed, if the store had a front porch, as many of them did, the kerosene pump was often kept there.

Southern Indians had preserved food before the coming of the colonists, and afterward fish was salted, beef "corned," and fruits dried or preserved in sugar. The process of canning foods was invented in France about 1795, and about 1815, when the "tin can" was developed, commercial canning became possible. Salmon and lobster, in particular, were sold in cans. Canned goods were expensive, however, until about the turn of the century; then processes were developed for manufacturing the cans cheaply. From that time forth a well-stocked grocery store had almost anything available in cans, and southerners ate more and more canned foods. Commercially dried fruits, especially apples, peaches, and apricots, also were to be had at relatively low prices, and they became an important part of the diet of many families. Probably a greater proportion of southern people ate dried fruits after the Civil War, when they were easily bought, than before, when each household did its own drying.

Foods canned at home were even cheaper than commercially canned foods. Housewives had preserved fruits in crockery jars, usually with sugar, since the colonial period, but easily sealed glass jars became available for home "canning" about the turn of the century. Home canning of fruits and vegetables, and sometimes meats, became much easier and more reliable when the coming of the pressure cooker made it possible to apply much more heat to the materials canned and thus more surely destroy bacteria that caused spoilage.[1] My mother, when her four children were all at home and possessed of large appetites, canned more than five hundred jars of fruits and vegetables a year; very few of them survived unopened until garden produce began to ripen the next spring.

Even so, the most striking fact about the diet of the New South, from the Civil War through World War II, is not that it changed, but how little it changed. Until I went away to war in 1942, I ate far more like my ancestors of the 1830s than the way I eat today. If the South was conservative in mores and politics, it was equally conservative in diet. Changes came slowly and grudgingly, and the dishes that southerners had been eating for more than a century were the most appreciated. A newly married couple did not need elaborate equipment to set up housekeeping. The essentials were a few cane-bottomed chairs, perhaps one rocking chair, an iron bedstead with springs and a mattress, a chest of drawers, a safe with tin doors (probably ventilated with nail holes), a cooking stove, some pots and pans and a few plates, cups, saucers, knives, spoons, and forks, a wash pan, a mirror, a washtub, an iron pot for heating water and rendering lard outdoors, and very little more.[2]

Southerners continued to eat corn bread, and as the years passed, good cooks became more and more sophisticated in their variations on the theme. The simple corn meal and water mixture did not fade away, though in the area of my youth it was baked with a little salt and called dog bread. From this stove-baked equivalent of the hoecake of antebellum days to the more sophisticated pones that included shortening and might include sugar, milk, eggs, and even flour, there must have been at least twenty-five easily distinguishable variations. One of the best was "hushpuppies," balls of corn bread batter flavored with onions among other things and cooked quickly in the hot grease in which fish had just been fried; but all corn bread was good to a southern palate. Rupert Vance found in the mid 1930s that the average southern family consumed five hundred pounds of cornmeal a year as compared to about one hundred pounds in the rest of the country. Obviously cornbread did not vanish from the southern menu, though there were some Yankees who wondered why not.[3]

As noted earlier, a practical commercial baking powder had been developed and placed on the market before the Civil War. Soon after the war the flour-milling industry achieved true mass production in the Middle West, producing white flour much more cheaply than a southern farmer could grow wheat and mill it into flour on his own land. Thereafter, for those who could afford them, biscuits took preference over corn bread most of the time. With sour milk one used baking soda, almost always Arm and Hammer brand, and with sweet milk baking powder. Eventually one could buy self-rising flour, with baking powder already mixed in, but the best cooks preferred to begin with plain flour.[4] Thus the simple ingredients of biscuits were flour, baking powder or soda, sweet or sour milk (sometimes buttermilk), hog lard as shortening, and a pinch of salt. But all biscuits were not alike; one of my grandmothers used much shortening and a minimum of baking powder, producing biscuits that were rather flat, slightly crisp, humble, and delicious beyond measure. The other grandmother made tall and arrogant biscuits, equally delicious. Whether from necessity or preference, my mother's biscuits fell somewhere in between, and they were just as good.

A southerner who matured in time for World War II could fill many pages with praise of the biscuit. Many families ate them three times a day; everyone of substance that I knew ate them for breakfast. They were excellent with butter and nothing else, but adding sorghum syrup or cane molasses made them better, as did some sort of homemade preserves or jelly. They were fine with flour gravy made from pork grease or, especially, from the grease left over after chicken had been fried. They were just as good, or even better, with red-eye gravy, made by pouring a little water into the pan with the hot grease left from frying ham or bacon. If some biscuits were left from supper, they could be halved and toasted with a bit of butter for breakfast. Hungry children ate them cold; I often carried three or four cold biscuits in my pocket so as to be prepared if the pangs of hunger struck too far from home. There are cooks who make such biscuits today, but one must be careful in restaurants; concoctions that come ready-mixed or, even worse, in cans cannot stand comparison with the biscuits of yesteryear.[5]

Cities, and some of the larger towns, had commercial bakeries long before the Civil War, but the majority of southern house-wives, if they wanted "light bread," had to make it, and it was a great deal more trouble to prepare than biscuits or corn bread. On the other hand, it was almost worth it, not only because it was good but also because, baking, it filled a whole house with a won-derful smell. In the 1920s small-town and country stores began to carry commercial bread, brought out from the nearest city in trucks, and soon it was presliced. It was something new; it was convenient; and it was cheap. I seem to remember ten cents a loaf. It became the supper bread for most town families and some farm ones, and as more housewives were influenced by women's maga-zines and home economics courses, toast rather than biscuits be-came breakfast fare. In defense of those who yielded, it should be noted that store bread then was much better than now; today a bag of air and chemicals mixed with a little flour, a loaf of commercial bread can be crushed to the size of an egg by any man with a good grip.

Probably southerners ate a greater proportion of pork to other meats for the eighty years following the Civil War than they had eaten during the preceding century. Those who raised their own hogs probably ate about the same quality of meat that their fathers and grandfathers had eaten; but black and white sharecroppers who depended upon the commissary or the general store, and yeoman farmers and denizens of the small towns who did not cure their own meat, lived on low quality bacon or fatback from the Middle West. Most of these unfortunate people, however, would be among the poor southerners whose diet is discussed in the next chapter. Southerners with the slightest degree of economic independence and initiative raised and slaughtered their own hogs, preserved in salt what could be preserved, then smoked it and hoped that it would last until the next hog killing. These people ate meats other than pork, as will be seen, but mainly they ate pork. In fact, meat and pork were synonyms, and it would almost be accurate to say that meat and bacon were synonyms; if a southerner meant ham, shoulder, or jowls, he would say so.

Hog-killing day was still one of the most important days of the year. It was of necessity a cold day, and one's hands, wet from scraping the porker's bristles after the carcass had been scalded, turned blue and lost their strength. When the carcass was hung up and the belly opened to remove the edible organs and offal from the interior, it was a pleasure almost sinful to thrust one's frigid hands into the still-warm abdominal cavity. As in earlier times, an orgy of pork eating followed slaughter, in which those parts that could not be preserved were eaten. People ate liver, brains, feet, backbone, loin, tails, ears, snouts, and chitterlings before they could spoil. One who watches newspaper advertisements closely will see ears, tails, and chitterlings advertised today by groceries located in the poorer sections of southern cities; food habits formed in the country generations ago still persist, despite a radical change in environment.

Fat was still rendered into lard in a huge cast-iron pot over a wood fire, and cracklings still were left to be mixed with cornmeal batter and baked into delectable crackling bread. When a family ran out of its own lard and went to the store for more, it much preferred hog lard to shortenings with a vegetable base. Scraps were still ground into sausage, and quarrels raged between and within families as to how much sage and how much black and red pepper should go into the final product. One of my grandfathers, a somewhat stubborn man who liked red pepper, threw a handful into his sausage, despite my grandmother's suggestion that he might be mixing in too much. Family legend has it that he was forced to kill and grind up major portions of two more hogs before he tamed his sausage down to the point that anyone born north of the Rio Grande could eat it.

Ham was at the apex of porkdom. Country-cured ham still has a mild vogue in the United States, and almost every southern state boasts a country ham better than any other. In the New South, Smithfield hams from Virginia probably had the highest reputation, but Tennessee hams from the Nashville area were also held in high regard. A farmer who did not take high pride in his hams was likely to plow a crooked furrow, and to bake half a ham for a guest was about as high an honor as one could pay. Country-cured hams were not, and are not, alike, but generally they were much saltier than hams from the midwestern slaughterhouses, and the meat was not nearly so fat. Now and then when I was a boy, nearly always in the summer or early fall after the meat had run out and before it was cold enough to kill more, my father would bring home a ham from the store. They were always better than the "sow bosom" on which we had been surviving, but they lacked the character of the hams we smoked in late December or early January. Nothing in all the culinary arts was better, on a crisp morning, than a fried slice of country ham with fried eggs, biscuits, red-eye gravy, molasses, butter, and black coffee, all combined with the appetite of a sixteen-year-old.[6]

From the end of the Civil War until long after the turn of the century, southerners certainly did not eat more beef than before the war, and it is probable that they ate less. Technically, they ate hardly any beef at all; bred cattle were rare, and the scrubs who shifted for themselves from the end of the harvest until spring planting began were as poor and as tough as the woods cattle of antebellum days. Before World War II, a few venturesome souls were beginning to breed true beef cattle, nearly always Herefords, but it was rarely that one of these strange short-legged creatures was slaughtered in the neighborhood. They were too good for southerners to eat and were sold to the operators of northern fat-tening pens. Southerners killed and ate calves and yearlings of their own scrub stock, animals that had not lived long enough to become truly tough. Somehow these creatures were cut into round steak, roasts, and soup bones, and nothing else. Roasts were cooked atop the stove in a roasting pan with a little water and perhaps some vinegar. Steaks were beaten to tenderize them and then fried.

Like beef, mutton probably came to the table less often after the Civil War than before, and it had never been a popular meat. I was fortunate enough never to taste mutton until I was on liaison duty with a British-Indian brigade in Burma in 1944; and I have never voluntarily eaten it since. Lamb chops are now fairly common, but in the supermarket they still are greatly outnumbered by the pork chops. The only other four-legged domestic animal ever devoured was the goat, usually in the form of barbecued kid. If done well, with a good sauce, it was not bad, but it was not something for which one would walk many miles.

Poultry was favored meat in the New South as it had been in the Old, but turkey and goose had become holiday fare. Southerners still did not eat guinea fowl in any numbers, and squab were not popular outside of south Louisiana. Some people had ducks, and duck eggs were eaten when available, but the birds themselves seldom came to the table. My grandparents kept ducks, but the first domestic duck I ever ate was a supposed Peking duck at a Chinese restaurant in Calcutta. So only chicken was left. Mature hens came to the table from time to time; during the depression a housewife's pride might be measured by whether she would kill a laying hen for guests when frying-size fowl were not to be had. Even a superannuated rooster could be boiled, diced, and made into chicken salad. But southerners preferred fried chicken, and fried chicken is what they ate when they could get it. They did not get it too often; it was a luxury food reserved for Sundays and other special days. Also, since nearly everyone depended upon hens to hatch the eggs and look after the chicks, the supply of fryers was largely dependent upon the seasons. I, for one, find it eminently satisfactory today that chicken is one of the most economical foods on sale and that new methods and new feeds have made fryers available any day of the year. Of course these modern chickens do not taste quite as good as those self-reliant birds of fifty years ago, but what does?[7]

Game and fish did not lose their place in the southern diet after the Civil War. Venison and wild turkey had become more and more rare as the forests were cleared away, but well into the twentieth century they were an important part of the diet of families in parts of east Texas. In some areas there, in fact, bear were killed, cured, and eaten like pork, almost as they had been eaten in the eighteenth-century frontier. Waterfowl were killed and devoured in abundance by those who lived on the flyways, but almost every year the numbers of ducks and geese seemed smaller, as commercial hunters killed them by the thousands and the expansion of agriculture in Canada and the northern states wiped out breeding grounds.

Most of the game of the New South was small game, but there was much of it, and it was eaten with gusto. Quail, or bobwhite, thrived in the honeysuckle fence rows, blackberry tangles, and sedge-grass fields of the impoverished New South. Very little land was posted, and anyone willing to make the effort to train a pointer or setter puppy could enjoy quail hunting such as can be had today only by Yankee millionaires and owners of large tracts of land. The millionaires, in fact, are often shooting pen-reared birds that have been whirled around to make them so dizzy that they will stand point. Limits were generous, but no southern gentleman, and no sensible hunter, ever killed all the birds in a covey. Few foods available to man were better than quail, especially for breakfast with biscuits and rich flour gravy.

Hunters here and there killed snipe and woodcock, and a few people, usually oldsters, illegally killed and ate robins. Even fewer killed blackbirds (actually grackles) and ate blackbird pie. The only other bird hunted on a large scale was the mourning dove, a few ounces of fine meat that could outspeed or dodge twice his weight in shot until the day he grew old or careless. Squirrels provided a favorite dish as well as a favorite sport; parboiled and then fried, cooked with flour dumplings, made into a broth, or providing the base of a rich Brunswick stew, they contributed to the good life. Coons were becoming scarce (there are far more of them about today than there were in the 1930s), but they could test any hound and were a favorite dish with many families. The possum also was not so abundant as in earlier years, not yet having learned how to survive as an urban animal, but there were still more possums than coons, they were easier to catch, and with sweet potatoes they were better to eat.

Without question, however, the cottontail rabbit was the most important game animal in the South, though his larger relative, the "swamp rabbit," was acceptable if he happened to show himself within shotgun range. Rabbit population was cyclical, but even in bad years they could be found in the same sort of terrain in which quail thrived. In years of high population they were so numerous that during the fall and winter a fair shot could give his family rabbit several times a week from one reasonably large and grassy cornfield. During the depression, rabbits were a vitally important part of the diet of many southerners. My father, sister, and I once tracked down and killed twenty-six cottontails after a snow, and every one of them was eaten by family, friends, or neighbors within two days.

Fish, as always, were most important along the Atlantic and Gulf coasts, but southerners everywhere ate fish when they could get them. Until World War II some were still preserved by salting for family use on the Atlantic Coast, and stores in the interior stocked salt mackerel from time to time, especially at Christmas. After the turn of the century canned sardines, salmon, and oysters became more and more common; salmon, indeed, became a cheap food, cooked in many ways but more often fried in croquettes or eaten as it came from the can. Even in the interior South, however, fish fresh from the water were preferred, and though other kinds were eaten with gusto, catfish was still best of all. There may have been southerners who baked or broiled freshwater fish, but they were few. Southerners believed that God made fish to be fried, and that is the way they came to the table. If some hushpuppies came with them, so much the better.

Rarer were such dishes as terrapin soup in Maryland and Virginia, and turtle soups and steaks in Georgia and South Carolina. Turtles went into the pot everywhere, but in Florida and south Georgia the little "cooter" was a favorite, and in Louisiana almost any turtle converted into turtle sauce piquant was a gourmet treat. Eels were eaten over much of the South, usually fried like any other fish. Frog legs were another delicacy, and huge bullfrogs still bellowed away in the South's many lakes, swamps, and creeks. Frog legs were almost as good as quail. Oysters, as indicated, were canned, but during the cold months they were still shipped far into the interior in the shell. Even so, away from the coast and bays, oysters au naturel were not so popular as they had been before the Civil War. Shrimp were not taken far into the interior, and crabs were nearly always boiled and eaten near where they were caught. Crayfish were then, as is largely the case now, eaten only in south Louisiana.[8]

Probably the milch cow was more important in the New South than in the Old. A family simply could not live decently without a cow; a reasonably prosperous family had enough cows to keep at least one of them fresh all year, so that the table need never be without milk. Cows were not restricted to the country; most small-town families also were dependent upon them. As necessary as they were, however, cows were nasty, brutish creatures. They had to be milked twice a day, which drastically limited the radius of social activity, especially for teen-age milkers. Cows had nasty habits; their tails were annoying weapons when they swished at flies; they were prone to kick without warning; and none of them were housebroken. Some kickers could be restrained by chains or ropes with metal hitches, and a skilled milker could place his head in a cow's flank and butt her off balance when he felt the muscles gathering for a kick. I once acquired a colony of large and ravenous lice from a cow so foiled.

The vegetables of the New South were basically the same as those of the Old. Tomatoes assumed more importance as more and more people, white and black, realized that they were not poisonous. Green corn, grits, Irish potatoes, sweet potatoes, cowpeas, and turnips remained the most important vegetables. The turnip hill and the sweet potato hill were expected sights in any comfortable farmer's backyard. Some entrepreneurs built potato houses and charged neighbors money or a part of their potatoes for protection. Most people, however, kept their sweet potatoes in hills or in their homes; I remember my grandfather, long white beard hanging outside his long white nightgown, as he went through his house on freezing nights, keeping up the fires in wood-fueled heaters to protect the sweet potatoes stacked in tall bushel baskets against the walls. As for the importance of cowpeas, one of my uncles, asked what he would do if a tornado threatened his hill-top house, answered that he would jump into the pea barrel that had kept him alive for two years and might be trusted for the future.

There were other vegetables—squash, onions, eggplant, peppers, okra, carrots, and parsnips to name a few. Some pretentious folk even had asparagus beds. Beans were loved as they had been since found in Indian patches. The butterbean, preferred green but happily cooked even if it was dry, was a favorite, as it still is and still deserves to be. Green beans were probably more popular. For most of the New South period, southern housewives continued to cook vegetables as they always had, boiling them for hours in a pot with a piece of fat salt pork. Cabbage so cooked drew flies by the hundreds and seemingly by the tens of thousands. In the 1920s and even more in the 1930s the home economics teachers and the home demonstration agents began to change the way vegetables were cooked. The amount of grease was reduced, so was the time in the pot. As a result the "pot likker," which, with corn bread, had been one of the most nutritious dishes on the southern table, began to fall into neglect. Not all agreed with this trend toward Yankee cooking; my father objected to green beans that practically snapped in one's mouth instead of submitting quietly to mastication, and he insisted that a good pot of beans had to have enough grease in it to wink back when winked at.

Fruits became less important after the Civil War than they had been before. The plantation owner had little or no incentive to grow fruit for sharecroppers as he had grown it for slaves. The orchard, in fact, almost disappeared from the commercial plantation and was confined to the land of the provident yeoman farmer. As the twentieth century wore on, those who grew apples, peaches, grapes, plums, and other orchard products found insects and fungus taking a heavier and heavier toll. In fact, one could almost say that "organic" orchards had failed even before they had been named. But for those families who had orchards, fruit, fresh and home canned, could be an important part of the diet. Faster transportation made citrus fruits available to much of the South regularly and to practically every household for Christmas, but these were exotics, coming from Florida or Texas. Sad to say, most of the apples sold in southern stores were produced in the North or in the Shenandoah Valley, but most of the peaches, at least, were of Deep South origin.

Watermelons and cantaloupes were produced on the lands of yeoman farmers rather than on planters' broad acres. What a treat a spring-cooled Black Spanish watermelon was on a hot August afternoon! A cool "mush melon" for breakfast was almost as good. Wild fruits and nuts continued to be important. Probably, as more and more forest was cleared away, blackberries and dewberries were more abundant than ever, and thrifty families braved redbugs and snakes to gather them for preserves, jam, jelly, pies, for eating raw with cream and sugar, and for making tart wine. The nuts were the same as ever, except that blight was gradually destroying the American chestnut and that the pecan, domesticated and improved, was beginning to have commercial importance in some parts of the South.[9]

For what it may be worth, I have formed the impression (without any quantitative evidence worth citing) that the middle-income southern farmers and townsmen had recovered from the Civil War by the beginning of the twentieth century and were as well off as ever before in southern history. Probably this resulted more from improved technology and communications than from self-sufficiency, but all of Henry Grady's exhortations did not fall on deaf

ears. Poor southerners, it must be emphasized, did not share in
this abundance, and there were many poor. But for those in decent
circumstances meals were hearty indeed. Rupert Vance noted that
a small farmer's breakfast was likely to be biscuits, coffee, salt or
smoked bacon, usually eggs, and in many instances milk, butter,
and cereal of some kind, most commonly grits. A well-to-do farmer
had much the same, but probably ham more often than bacon, and
it was very likely accompanied by fruit, jam, preserves, milk, and
butter. One yeoman family in north Louisiana always had hot
biscuits, butter, molasses, fried meat, and gravy. Ben Robertson reported of his youth in up-country South Carolina: "At breakfast we
had a big bowl of water-ground hominey grits. . . . We never
missed having . . . [grits] and we never tired of it, and we could eat
it, and we did eat it, every morning of every year. . . . We had red
gravy in bowls and wide platters filled with thick slices of
ham . . . and we had fried eggs right from the nests. We had pitch-
erfuls of rich milk . . . . and we had blackberry jam for the hot
biscuits."[10] Incidentally, grits were not eaten throughout all the
New South. The first time I ever saw them was during World War II
on a train from Miami to Nashville.

Breakfasts were substantial, but the noon meal was yet the most
important one of the day. Dinner was usually more abundant and
more elaborate on Sundays than on other days, but it had to be a
sustaining meal for hard-working people every day of the week.
The small farmer's dinner might have no meat except that cooked
with vegetables, accompanied by as much corn bread as the family
could eat and perhaps by milk. Vance found most small farmers
eating corn bread and pork boiled with beans, peas, Irish potatoes,
collards, or other greens. About one-third had fried meat, and
about as many had canned fruit. Most of them drank milk, some
drank coffee, and many had only water. None ate beef, steak, raw
fruit, sauerkraut, carrots, spinach, veal, seafood, or white bread
other than biscuits. The well-to-do farmers surveyed by Vance ate
much corn bread and Irish potatoes, but they ate less boiled meat
and more fried. Half of the tables had canned vegetables and
canned fruit. "The proportion of desserts is double that in the

menu of small farm owners, and most significant, fruit and vegetable salads appear on almost 42 percent of the tables. Roast beef for
the first time gains an important place, appearing on the menu of 20
percent, and is matched by fried chicken in the same ratio."[11]

In upland South Carolina, "we had soup and two or three kinds
of meat, fried chicken, fried ham, or spareribs or liver pudding,
and we had four or five vegetables and a dessert or so, and
fruit. . . . I don't think I ever had all the fried chicken I could eat
until I was twenty-one. . . . We liked ducks next to chicken and
sometimes ate a goose or turkey, but it never occurred to us to eat a
guinea fowl." A man who grew up in north Louisiana remembered
"Deep oblong china dishes . . . set at intervals along the cloth-cov-
ered table. These were filled with peas, string beans, okra, squash,
beets, turnip greens or collards in the spring and late fall, scraped
kernels of field corn cooked in milk and butter at green shuck
time. . . . The vegetables were cooked fresh in season or emptied
from glass Mason jars and heated at other times." Carl Carmer
took special note of meals he ate in Alabama, ranging from "pork
chops and sweet potatoes and collards" with poor people in south
Alabama, through "chicken and dumplings, sweet potato pie, ham
from the smokehouse, corn bread in large pones, scrambled eggs,
snap beans, biscuits and cane syrup, and a goblet of buttermilk at
each plate" in the northern part of the state. Eating was even better in the black belt where "a ham and a chicken and a roast are
served with corn and okra and snap beans, cowpeas, and collard
greens, and sweet potatoes, beaten biscuit and corn bread, a salad
and a watermelon, for just a 'pick-up potluck dinner.'"[12]

For poor farmers, supper was a very light meal, usually made up
of left-overs from dinner plus corn bread. If there were no leftovers, the housewife might cook biscuits and fry bacon. Better-off
farmers also ate leftovers, but often with the addition of hot corn
bread or biscuits, fried meat, and eggs.[13] One man brought up in
the rural South remembered supper as "a hasty, unimportant meal
of cold and unappetizing leftovers, with occasionally a dish of fruit
in season or jam of some kind to supplement the syrup. Sometimes
after we got an icebox we drank tall glasses of iced tea, heavily

sugared." Ben Robertson remembered: "Often all we would have would be milk . . . . cornbread, sliced thin and almost sizzling hot; soft salted fresh butter; and sorghum molasses. Soon after supper we washed our feet and went to bed. We believed we slept better if at our last meal we had eaten but little." Colonel James Monroe Smith, reportedly the richest man in Georgia, had a somewhat more elaborate supper. One winter night his table bore "beef steak, country ham, batter cakes, hot biscuits, preserves, and syrup." Perhaps it should be mentioned, too, that the colonel weighed close to three hundred pounds.[14]

9

Eating, Drinking, and Socializing
THE NEW SOUTH, CONTINUED

The diet of southerners who lived in towns and villages after the Civil War did not differ much from that of their relatives who remained on the farm. The towns and cities increased in size, but their inhabitants were in the main rural people. In the smaller places, every family of any status kept one or more cows, chickens, and hogs for fattening and killing when winter came. Hunting small game was little if any more difficult for the man who lived in town than it was for the farmer. Townsmen also planted gardens. It is my impression—I certainly have no statistical evidence—that a larger proportion of the families living in towns than of families living in the country had gardens. Many town dwellers also had small orchards for home use. They did eat more canned goods, and more store-bought food in general, than thrifty yeoman farmers, but they were nonetheless heavily dependent upon their gardens and their animals.

The relatively small proportion of southerners who lived in true cities did not have the opportunities for gardening and animal husbandry that existed in small towns, but swill dairies, dairies that fed penned cows on mash from distilleries and sold the milk fresh, presumably existed in southern cities, as they certainly did in the North. Some city dwellers kept milkers until well after the turn of the century. I had little trouble finding a cow for a fraternity prank in Memphis in the late 1930s. In the 1950s I had neighbors in Montgomery, Alabama, who kept chickens for both meat and eggs. But the city family nonetheless bought a great deal more from the grocery than did the resident of a village. He bought canned goods and some fresh meat, but to a remarkable extent he bought what he would have grown for himself had he been on a farm: cured pork, sweet potatoes, beans, Irish potatoes, turnips, cowpeas, molasses, and canned tomatoes. To these items he probably would add canned beans, salmon, and oysters, salt fish on occasion, and in the twentieth century, canned soups. Probably these city dwellers were losing some southern characteristics, but certainly not rapidly.

In general southerners were not inclined toward "eating out," though there were excellent restaurants in Baltimore, Charleston, Savannah, New Orleans, and a few other cities after the Civil War as well as before. One Yankee, soon after the war, was not impressed. He reported from Charleston that he had had salt fish, fried potatoes, and treason for breakfast; fried potatoes, treason, and salt fish for dinner; treason, salt fish, fried potatoes, and a little more treason for supper. Most of the time in the New South, as in the Old, the traveler or the southerner away from home could expect bad victuals if he found himself in a southern town where he had no friends or relatives in whose home he could eat. As late as the 1950s the ordinary motorist could find all too few good eating places between Baton Rouge and Charleston. Breakfast might be edible, though probably overgreasy; later in the day a ham sandwich was the safest thing to order.[1]

There were honorable exceptions. Carl Goerch enjoyed a seventy-five-cent dinner in a Yancey County, North Carolina, hotel, served home style, which was almost Lucullan. It included country sausage, backbone, spareribs, roast turkey, big hominy, sauerkraut, coleslaw, turnips, sweet potatoes, Irish potatoes, corn bread, blackeye peas, prunes, biscuits, baked beans, relish, sliced pickles, honey, ice cream, preserves, jellies, cake, coffee, tea, and milk. Near Caesar's Head, South Carolina, Jonathan Daniels discovered a restaurant that for forty cents gave him rib stew, eggplant, spinach, potatoes, custard pie, and coffee, all good. Another hungry traveler was delighted with the ham, okra, tomatoes, hot biscuits, corn bread, butter, honey, collard greens, and pecan pie he was served in a Peachtree Street restaurant in Atlanta. Scattered all over the South were places, some terrible but many good, which served almost nothing but catfish and hushpuppies. These meals were much better than the food Daniels got at the Community House of TVA's Norris Dam, which "was as inexpensive, healthy and as uninteresting as food always is when dieticians are in charge."[2]

Water continued to be the South's favorite drink. More and more, in towns, it came from a faucet, but the vast majority of southerners after the Civil War got their water from wells, mostly shallow. Even after 1900, most of them were dug with pick and shovel, and the well digger, unless he was a drunkard, which seems often to have been the case, was a man whose courage earned him respect. How near it was to the well was an important factor in determining the desirability of a house, but even if the well was on the back porch, which was a great blessing, human arms still had to bring the water from the depths. Drawing water for a family's needs—drinking, cooking, washing, and now and then bathing—was onerous enough, but if cattle and hogs also had to be watered, then one was indeed sentenced to hard labor. One historian suggests that "it was by the side of the back country wells that much of southern womanhood lost both beauty and health."[3] Perhaps this was true, but in my memory it was boys who drew most of the water. Wooden buckets were used until about 1920, but when narrow, bored wells replaced the dug well, long metal cylinders replaced the buckets. Cedar buckets were favorite containers, and everyone drank from a common dipper. It might be a gourd, carved from wood, or metal manufactured for the purpose. Water from every well had an individual taste; a man who got about the neighborhood could probably identify the water from one of a dozen or more wells with a sip. However one's water tasted, hard, soft, sulfurous (just a tiny bit), one much preferred it to the characterless liquid drunk by those who, unable to find underground water, depended upon a cistern to catch rainwater.

Whether because coffee was cheaper than before the Civil War or for some other reason, almost all adults drank it for breakfast, and many families for other meals. People who could not afford sugar still drank black coffee. One bought beans in the store, roasted them in the kitchen oven to one's own taste, and then ground them in an arm-powered home grinder. Most coffee was roasted to a light or medium complexion and then boiled, but the percolator was becoming more and more popular. In south Louisiana and Alabama the beans were roasted until very dark and then ground fine; then hot water was dripped very slowly through the grounds to make coffee fit for the gods. Outsiders who could not understand how such wonderful aroma could come from coffee alone insisted that chicory was added, but that was not a common practice then or now.

Upper-class southerners had drunk hot tea before the Civil War, and no doubt iced tea had been enjoyed here and there. In the upper South ice was gathered from lakes and ponds in winter and stored in insulated icehouses for summer use, and ships brought ice from the North into southern ports. Iced tea really became popular, however, when machinery for making ice became available, and even fairly small towns could support an icehouse. Iced tea, improved by lemon and sugar, became the southerner's favorite summer drink, and it is hard to imagine anything better. The waste involved in transporting ice from town to farm on a summer day in a buggy or wagon limited enjoyment of this fine drink by farm families until the internal combustion engine brought the automobile to country roads. The T-Model or one of its successors could rush a block of ice from town to farm for tea or even for making homemade ice cream on a hot day. Soon enterprising men had regular ice routes that delivered to the farms in their area. Then, in the late 1920s and early 1930s, the electric refrigerator appeared, and the TVA and rural electrification made it possible for the farm family to use this truly great convenience. It was probably more appreciated for the ice cubes it provided for tea than for any of its other services.

Nonalcoholic commercial drinks go far back in American history, but the soft drink did not really come into its own until the twentieth century. The Coca Cola made a few Georgians wealthy and, selling for five cents, conquered all the United States and invaded many foreign nations. Jonathan Daniels concluded in the 1930s, probably correctly, that there was no place in the South that the drink had not penetrated. Perhaps because it tasted so good, perhaps because the early version was believed to have a faint trace of cocaine among its ingredients, the drink was looked upon in some areas as mildly sinful. Children, especially, were urged to drink grape, orange, or other-flavored carbonated drinks. Most of those who could afford it nonetheless went through a stage of near addiction to Coca Cola. Before World War II, other cola drinks were on the market.[4]

Outside of Louisiana, only well-to-do southerners, and not nearly all of them, had been wine drinkers before the Civil War, and wine drinking was even less prevalent in the widespread poverty that followed the sectional struggle. Beer had never been one of the South's favorite drinks, and since there was no large German migration into the South in the 1840s, beer did not grow in popularity as it did in the Middle West. The one exception, again, was New Orleans, where many Germans did settle. The drinking of beer was on the increase when prohibition went into effect, and southerners tried their hand at home brew along with the rest of the nation; but under prohibition, as before, southerners who drank usually sought something stronger than beer. It was not until the repeal of the Eighteenth Amendment that today's affinity between beer and the southern climate led to the litter that may cause some future archaeologist to denominate this the beer-can age.

Whiskey was as available after the Civil War as before. Liquor of some quality on which taxes had been paid could be had in hotels, saloons, and country stores. Indeed, protection of the whiskey barrel was a problem in rural and small-town stores because thieves yearned for it more than for anything else. One way of stealing whiskey was to bore a hole upward through the floor into the barrel, then catch the liquid in buckets. To prevent this the whiskey barrel was often put on blocks or otherwise raised as far as feasible from the floor.

Legally, the South was drying up long before prohibition. The temperance movement led to local option, and in many towns and counties the Baptists, Methodists, and bootleggers were numerous enough to vote to close the legal outlets. Eventually, of course, the Eighteenth Amendment theoretically did away with drinking completely. What it really did, in the South, was to make it possible for enterprising bootleggers to make sizable fortunes; almost any southerner past sixty can name some families in his locality who today have the social status to mingle with the best, and whose position is based on a fortune accumulated largely by bootlegging. Unfortunately, all but a very few of them made whiskey of much lower quality than the illegal free enterprise distilleries of earlier times. Mash made from a peck of sprouted corn, fifty pounds of sugar, water, and yeast would ferment much more rapidly than all-grain mash, and fifty gallons would produce up to five gallons of moonshine whiskey. It was strongly recommended that this filthy and fiery stuff be twice filtered through charcoal to remove the head-splitting impurities, but this precaution was often neglected.

Carl Carmer concluded, after drinking corn whiskey for six years whenever the occasion rose, that it was "as vile and as uglily potent a liquor as ever man has distilled. It is swift and deadly— odious to the taste." I am old enough to have watched moonshine in the making and have tasted the first hot drops from the worm. I drank it when nothing else was available. Most of it was as terrible as Carmer says, but some was almost 150 proof, pure as rainwater, clear as crystal, and a more potent tranquilizer than any modern tablet or capsule.[5]

Southerners did not visit as much after the Civil War as before; few could afford the kind of hospitality that had characterized social-minded planters, and all classes had to pay closer attention to the work, agricultural or otherwise, that put food on the table. Even so, southerners probably visited more than other Americans. One type of visiting was a tragic result of the war. That struggle had left a hundred thousand or more widows and perhaps as many or more women who as a result of the slaughter were never married. This condition did not correct itself in one generation; it continued on for two or more.

In the nineteenth century, and in the South in the early twentieth, there were few ways for a woman to support herself. A great many of these southern women without men survived largely by "visiting" brothers and sisters, their own children if they had them, nieces and nephews, and old friends. They were not parasites; they helped with the housework, looked after the children, and if the hostess was young, they taught her the feminine skills they had learned over a lifetime. All of them that I remember were beloved by the children of the families they visited. Looking back over the years, I can now see that they had an exquisite sense of timing, knowing exactly when to move on.

One should not conclude that the southern love of visiting and being visited had atrophied; it was merely modified by circumstances. One observer in the Appalachians noted fairly recently that the mountaineer still believed it a point of honor to offer his roof, his table, and his drink to every caller. Upper-class Atlantans long after the Civil War opened their houses at noon on New Year's Day and kept them open until late in the evening. Anyone might walk in, present his card, and enjoy a glass of wine and a piece of cake. Obviously, an interloper too far down the social scale would not have a card. Carmer found that visiting was a "happy recreation" in Alabama during the 1920s and early 1930s, something which both the visitor and the host took very seriously. Also, he was impresssed by the length of some visits.[6] All over the South, after as well as before the Civil War, the following routine was commonly observed when church services were over.

> It was not unusual for half the congregation to go home with the others to eat late Sunday dinner. The cakes, pies, and meats—baked ham, turkey, roast pork—were already cooked and waiting . . . . for word that they were "expected" next Sunday would already have reached the ones to be invited. Only the chicken had to be fried, the biscuit cooked, and the huge pot of coffee boiled. It was

not at all against the principles of the most devout for the menfolk to
go to the smokehouse and uncork the wine barrel or the brown jug
to put a razor edge on the already sharp appetite.[7]

It is necessary to emphasize that in the New South as in the Old,
the householder's door was not open to all. In addition to the barri-
ers imposed by race, people of definitely lower social status were
not invited to visit, and they did not come. Strangers were looked
upon with suspicion. A *southern* couple moving into a new community lived in social isolation for years, unless, perhaps, the
husband had some position of authority. Their children, however,
especially nubile adolescents, might make friends much more
quickly than their parents if they had no socially unacceptable
characteristics. Perhaps it was a result of the surplus of women
after the Civil War, but boys were accepted more quickly than their
sisters. A family from the North was outcast for a longer time, especially if the head of the household happened to be a professing
Republican, but in this case also a position of economic power
could make a difference. Friends of friends were received, but
more or less on probation. In other words, the rules of hospitality
in the South after the Civil War were very much as they had been
for more than a century before the war.

Southerners still thoroughly enjoyed community or neighborhood gatherings for almost any purpose. Work gatherings did not
end with Appomattox. On the contrary, house-raisings, logrollings,
corn shuckings, and the like continued well into the twentieth
century; newspapers yet carry occasional stories of house-raisings, though the circumstances usually are out of the ordinary. If
the gathering was all white, women would be present to prepare
food, and they might have a quilting or some other activity for part
of the day. If some of the workers were black, the host would provide whiskey only, and the women would remain at home. The
supply of food could be stomach boggling. At a corn shucking in
Rowan County, North Carolina, the participants shared light bread,
biscuits, ham, fresh pork, chicken pie, cake, coffee, sweet milk
and buttermilk, and for sweetening, preserves. A logrolling before

or after secession could offer "a sixty gallon boiler filled with rice, chicken, and fresh pork backbone—a sort of camp stew; a large pot of turnip greens and corn meal dumplings, served with a boiled ham sliced and laid on top; crackling or shortening bread; Irish potatoes, sweet potatoes, a variety of cakes, two-story biscuits; and, of course, the huge pot of coffee."[8]

The barbecue, political or otherwise, did not come to an end with the war. Sometimes instead of a barbecue it was a picnic, where each family brought part of the food to be consumed. Perhaps because of General John C. Pemberton's surrender of Vicksburg on July Fourth, the whites in much of the South did not celebrate Independence Day. But in my youth the black people of our little community gathered each year on that day for a tremendous picnic in a well-shaded pasture. On the way they marched through our little hamlet with a drum aboard a two-horse wagon leading the way. Country stores were also a convenient place for barbecues, picnics, and all-day singings, any one of which was an occasion for good eating. In 1893 the wealthy Colonel Smith of Georgia gave a picnic for whites only, setting forth "gallons of snap beans, onions, potatoes, English peas and the like . . . and plenty of delicious pone bread to go with them; a pile of boiled sliced home-cured ham . . . a half bushel or more of superb light biscuits from home raised flour . . . light bread . . . good old-fashioned peach pie . . . a pile of apple pies stacked a foot or so high, and pickles and custards and cakes of many different kinds in almost endless profusion."[9]

The next year Colonel Smith enlarged his operation and gave a barbecue for fifteen hundred people, black and white, though carefully segregated. "Seventy-nine hogs were barbecued; 'wash pot after wash pot of hash' was prepared; two large two-horse wagon-loads of bread were brought out. . . . The feast ended with several hundred watermelons. After the white guests had eaten their fill, the colored guests were invited to come up, and after they had eaten to their satisfaction, there was still enough victuals to feed several hundred people."[10] The barbecue is far from dead. Political barbecues are still an essential part of campaigning for office in many parts of the South, and when diplomatic relations with China were restored, a southern president felt that the vice-premier of that Socialist nation needed to attend a Texas barbecue as part of his learning about the United States.

In the years soon after the Civil War, weddings were still occasions for happy gatherings at tables loaded with food, but gradually the gatherings died out, replaced to some extent by the much less satisfactory, and much more expensive, reception, often with catered food. Even the sad occasion of a death had its social and gastronomic side; until the funeral home became almost a necessity, the neighbors who sat up with the corpse were provided with ample food and, usually, whiskey. After the burial, those who called at the deceased's home could also expect to be offered food, often dishes brought in by the neighbors.

Other occasions for social gatherings were not neglected. Agrarian Herman Nixon tells that Possum Trot, Alabama, had "candy pullings, box suppers, breakdowns, and picnics, with kissing games and 'lemonade stirred with a spade.'" Box suppers offered excellent possibilities for good eating and socially approved courtship, but the same could be said for all-day singings and even revival camp meetings. Carl Carmer described the eating at an all-day singing: "The tops were off the boxes now, revealing great quantities of fried chicken, beaten biscuit, corn bread, pickles, preserves, white frosted cakes." At camp meetings good food was brought from home or cooked on the grounds, although nearby might still be found "another camp meeting . . . being conducted by Satan himself, where . . . the 'rowdy element' congregated to 'drink whiskey, smoke cigars, play cards'" and engage in other sinful activities.[11] A community or extended family gathering to clean the graveyard might also be the occasion for a picnic. Finally there was the community supper, not necessarily in honor of a special occasion, perhaps held to raise money for some worthy cause and offering the best food of the best cooks in the neighborhood.

Dinner on the grounds at rural southern churches was a cherished occasion for two generations after the Civil War, and it is a practice that has not yet yielded completely to the onrush of mod-

ernity. Such a dinner at the church of four generations of my ancestors recently afforded an array of foods not too different from
those served under the same trees fifty years ago: ham and fried
chicken in apparently limitless quantity; deviled eggs by the hundreds if not by the thousands; a bushel or more of coleslaw and as
much potato salad; and an astonishing array of cakes and pies. Of
course little if any of the ham and chicken was home reared; probably a careful inspection would have revealed that some of the
cakes and pies were commercial products, but most of them had
been made at home. A barrel of iced tea was available to wash
down this food; in addition, and this would not have been the case
fifty years ago, there were tubs of iced soft drinks for those who
preferred them.[12] After such a dinner, my mother always refused to
prepare any supper at all, maintaining that to add more food to such
a feast was bad for the health. As a result the rest of the family made
do very well with buttermilk and cold bread if any bread was on
hand, or with plain whole milk if that was all there was.

10

Fatback, Pellagra, and Clay Eaters

THE IMPOVERISHED SOUTH

Some southerners were so poverty stricken after the Civil War that they require separate treatment. Some of these unfortunates were the "poor whites" described by northern travelers before the war, but many were black, and as time passed, others were yeoman farmers or their sons who had become enmeshed in the cords of the crop lien system and were dragged down to abject poverty. The number of people caught in this trap seems to have increased constantly down to the 1930s, though some years were good when compared to others; economic conditions in general were at their worst in the 1870s, the 1890s, and the 1930s, but for the poor they were bad at all times.

The diet of the impoverished was affected by the technological changes noted earlier. As flour imported from the Northwest became cheap, biscuits were more frequently substituted for corn bread, but it must not be thought that corn bread disappeared from the table. Both flour and cornmeal ground by the new processes were less nutritious than they had been in earlier years. Less and less did the truly poor southerner kill his own hogs; he relied upon the general store or the plantation commissary to provide him with meat. This meat was more often fatback than bacon—such people seldom if ever tasted ham, shoulder, or sausage—and thus deficient in protein. Katherine du Pre Lumpkin noted that when she was attending a country school in the sand hills of eastern South Carolina, "my lunches were different. . . . It disturbed me to take from my kit at recess good beef or cheese sandwiches, a boiled egg, an apple, and piece of cake, and parade it before their heavy thick flour biscuit or corn bread, with at best a piece of fatback on it."[1]

Probably most undernourished southerners had sufficient calories, though many certainly did not; what they lacked were proteins and, especially, the vitamins that would have prevented the all too frequent cases of rickets and pellagra. To add to the tragedy of the impoverished, lack of sanitation and the habit of going barefoot in summer, and in winter too when people could not afford shoes, resulted in widespread intestinal worm infestation; these parasites, roundworms and hookworms, used up much of the food poor people ate. A southerner might eat his fill of fatback, corn bread or flour biscuit, and molasses and still be malnourished and undernourished.

It seems indisputable that the condition of the poor, whether sharecroppers in the black belt, millworkers in the Piedmont, or scratch farmers in Appalachia, began to reach its nadir about 1925. Long before panic hit Wall Street, many southern farmers had been depressed to such a point that things could hardly have been worse this side of the grave.[2] The low price of cotton and tobacco had forced many landlords to retire marginal land from cultivation. The displaced tenants, who might have been earning an entirely inadequate one hundred to two hundred dollars a year as sharecroppers, now become occasional laborers who earned less than one hundred dollars a year. The sharecropper spent almost three-fourths of his meager earnings for food, and he ate poorly. The tenant who was displaced obviously went hungry. Those few who were able to get on relief rolls after the New Deal began or to obtain jobs with the Works Projects Administration definitely improved their standard of living.[3]

The New Deal, World War II, and the generally prosperous generation from the end of that war to the late 1970s greatly reduced the number of impoverished people in the South if poverty is defined as the condition just described. One fact noted today by many southerners who grew up during the 1920s and 1930s is that the "poor white" has largely vanished from the rural countryside. Sometimes his descendants are prosperous bankers or merchants or landowners, and the weddings of his granddaughters and great-granddaughters receive much attention on the society pages of county newspapers. More often such poor families have moved to the cities, North and South, where their economic fortunes have varied. Some of them have prospered; most have survived as semi-skilled workers; and many are on the welfare rolls.

Poverty-stricken blacks do remain on the rural lands of the South, but not in nearly the numbers that existed before World War II. Displaced first by the agricultural depression of the 1920s, then by the crop reduction program of the New Deal, then by employment opportunities in the North and West as a result of World War II and its aftermath, and at long last by the mechanization of southern agriculture, black people, too, found their way to cities all over the nation. This "modern Enclosure Movement without parallel in the nation's history," as it was described by Herbert Gutman, probably improved the diet of most of the migrants, but it nonetheless left many of them in abject poverty within the big city ghettos.[4]

The diet of the poorest people in the New South was not completely different from that of those well off enough not to be considered poor. It had much less variety, however, and at times of the year it often simply was not enough in quantity. No hard and fast rules can be stated, but the wretchedly poor family almost never raised its own pork, had few if any chickens, had no cow or else had a gaunt beast that had trouble surviving the winter, and either had no garden at all or planted a few straggly rows that bore scantily in the spring and had to be quickly abandoned as the heat of summer bore down. Neighbors often looked upon them as "shiftless," which they were; but whether they were shiftless because they were poor and ill fed, or whether they were poor and ill fed because they were shiftless cannot be determined here.

Practically all their flour, cornmeal, hog lard, and molasses came from the store or commissary, bought on credit under the crop lien. One must not think that the tenant (or the yeoman farmer caught up in the system) could buy throughout the year, or that he could buy all he wanted at any time. The amount of his credit was fixed by the landlord or the merchant, and it seldom amounted to more than seven or eight dollars a month. Furthermore, this "furnish" was available for only part of the year; for four to six months the impoverished farm family had to shift for itself completely, and it was not unusual for a household to be reduced for weeks at a time to corn bread alone, or perhaps to sweet potatoes alone. Indeed, one Mississippi townsman was irritated when he discovered that the sharecropper family that kept his hunting dogs was eating the food, probably cornmeal, that he sent out for feeding the animals.[5]

Doleful descriptions of the diet of the southern poor are abundant, but they have a certain sameness about them. The "farmer jolted homeward behind a jaded pair of mules with a can of kerosene, a hunk of meat, a pail of . . . lard, and dust-covered bags of flour and meal. . . . At home wives sliced off thick pieces of the Iowa meat and fried it for breakfast, boiled hunks of it for dinner and fried more of it for supper. They thickened the gravy with flour and served it and molasses as sop for corn bread and biscuit. Three times a day and fifty-two weeks a year, for many, was a long monotonous year of meat, corn bread, biscuit, gravy and molasses." Actually, a family that had even this every day of the year was far better off than scores of thousands of other families, some of whom could afford Iowa fatback only two or three times a week.[6] One black man remembered: "Most any kind of meat was a treat to us. At hog killin' time we'd get a ration of meat for helpin' neighbors render their lard." In the 1960s Robert Coles ate with a white mountain family, getting "a meal of corn bread, pork that was just about all fat, and coffee without milk."[7]

There were a few variations on the basic diet. Some black families had not begun to use the cookstove and still ate from the common pot that hung in the fireplace. A black maid in Memphis in the 1930s marveled to "recollect how us Prentices had the grab habit at the table, most everything we had to eat all in one pot on the hearth or kitchen table, and now me steppin' round like a bird on sore claws, passin' eats one at a time." Even the poorest poor in south Louisiana managed to put together red beans or white beans and rice, often supplemented with fish or game. In the mill towns of the Piedmont and in the alluvial cotton-growing areas of eastern Arkansas, poor families learned to eat huge quantities of beans, and this may well have been true elsewhere in the South. No doubt they were much more nutritious than fatback.[8]

Even the poorest people had small luxuries now and then, though the husband who went to the gin and the store was more likely than his wife and children to sample bought items. If a poor family had a neighbor with a garden, frequently they would be invited to help themselves; gardening has always been feast or famine. Cowpeas preceded soybeans as a hay crop, and often poor people were allowed to pick and eat the green peas. They could have picked and stored more after they were dry, but they seldom did. Sometimes the very poor farmer was a hunter, but more than likely he sooner or later sold his gun. Even if he had one, he often could not buy shells. Some, known to be skilled, might "go halves" and divide the kill with a merchant who liked game enough to provide the ammunition. If he lived near a stream, the poor man might be a fisherman, but even at this he was likely to be unsuccessful; he could not afford good equipment, but he would not have known how to use it if he had had it. At the store, if he had a few coins or a little credit left, he might treat himself to a can of cove oysters or sardines, or a slice of cheese with salt crackers, and later on he might have a soft drink of some kind with it. He might also buy some raw corn whiskey and get roaring drunk, but that was another type of activity.[9]

There is less information on the food of poor people in the cities and towns of the New South than on the diet of their rural brethren. As noted, in small towns and to some extent in cities it was sometimes possible to have gardens and even to keep cows and chickens, and thus low income did not automatically condemn an urban family to an inadequate diet. In some cities "swill milk" was fairly cheap for those who could not keep cows. The women in many black families worked as domestic servants, and it was not at all unusual for them to "tote," that is, to bring leftovers from their employer's house home with them. When these women planned the meals, as they often did, the leftovers might be of good quality and considerable quantity. One gets the impression, without quantitative data, that the kind of abject poverty among urban blacks which my generation saw during the Great Depression began primarily with the arrival of displaced sharecroppers, already conditioned to semistarvation, in the cities in the late 1920s and early 1930s. On the other hand, malnourishment because of poverty seems to have been common among whites in cotton mill towns along the fall line from the turn of the century onward. Yet people still flocked into the mill towns from the worn-out little farms of the Piedmont.[10]

The fact that even in the best of years scores of thousands of families in the South quite literally lived on the edge of starvation perhaps explains why southerners who saw living conditions in Asia during World War II and afterward were not so upset as servicemen who came from more economically prosperous parts of the United States. They saw what they had been seeing all their lives, except on a larger scale. Probably the most impressive testimony to the conditions that existed among the southern poor is the fact that poor people fortunate enough to get on relief during the early days of the New Deal, at a time when money payments and commodity distribution did not amount to more than five or ten dollars a month at most, were still much better off than wage workers on plantations. Later, when Works Projects Administration jobs paid forty to fifty dollars a month, the fortunate poor southerner who "got on" WPA could probably be described as having moved out of the ranks of the truly impoverished. Welfare rolls in the South were highly restricted because the payments, though niggardly in comparison to those made in northern states, still enabled a family to eat a more satisfying diet than plantation laborers or sharecroppers could afford. Expanded welfare rolls might have reduced the labor supply and forced employers to pay higher wages.[11]

Southerners did not feel particularly imposed upon by the depression, because poverty was a way of life in the former Confederacy. "For a whole week one time we didn't have anything to eat but potatoes. Another time my brother went around to grocery stores and got them to give him meat for his dog—only he didn't have any dog." The same narrator went on, "Every now and then my brother or Dad would find some sort of odd job to do, or the other brother in Chicago would send us something. Then we'd go wild. I mean we'd go wild over food. We'd eat until we were sick. We'd eat four times a day and between meals." Harry Ashmore remembered the blacks of Greenville, South Carolina, "the swollen bellies of rickety children, the scabs of pellagra, the hollow cheeks of the tubercular. Yet there was an astonishing vitality, too, in the broad-shouldered bucks swinging off in the dawn to their muscle-straining jobs." Nor did southerners lose their sense of humor. One Texan, probably better off than many because he did have greens, said after the depression was a memory that he had no more appetite for collards. "I eat so many collard greens during the depression I had to wrap my ankles to keep the cut worms off."[12]

The suffering of the southern poor did not end with the depression, but the number of those who suffered was reduced greatly as poor families, black and white, left the land and moved to the cities. Even so, pockets of poverty as shocking as those that had existed during the 1930s and the 1870s were still to be found in Appalachia, in the hill country of Louisiana and Texas, in the Mississippi Delta, on the Sea Islands of South Carolina, and elsewhere. As late as 1966, about one-half of the poor families of the United States, one-seventh of the white poor and two-thirds of the nonwhite poor, lived in the South. In 1970 a county-by-county study of hunger ordered by Governor Ernest Hollings of South Carolina brought an estimate that 11 percent of the people of that state lacked enough to eat, and there is no reason to believe that similar surveys in other southern states would have shown significantly better conditions. Robert Coles noted near the same time that "Americans [in the South] go hungry every day, become malnourished, die because they don't get enough food and the right kind of food and fall sick and never, never at all see a doctor; American children possess bloated bellies and swollen ankles, even suffer from . . . diseases that mark the very last stages of starvation and that are associated with countries like Biafra or cities like Calcutta."[13]

The damage done to the poor people of the South by an inadequate diet for almost, if not entirely, a century cannot be expressed in monetary or qualitative terms, but it is terrible to contemplate. Children inadequately fed might suffer only a high incidence of tooth decay because of lack of calcium, but malnutrition can also bring about permanent brain damage. As is well known, there were people scattered throughout the South, and there probably still are, who eased the pangs of hunger by eating clay. People seeing the children of tenant families for the first time often noted how small they were for their ages. Observers also noted the slowness of their movements, which gave them every appearance of laziness beyond endurance. Yet more often than not they had no more energy to expend. Whether this was because they did not get enough to eat, or because intestinal worms were digesting a goodly share of what they did eat, really made little difference.[14]

The more optimistic among southerners have tended to look for quick solutions to the health problems brought on by hunger. At one time the antihookworm crusade of the Rockefeller Sanitary Commission was hailed as a near miracle that would make poor lazy southerners, black and white, over into energetic Yankees. The attempt to eradicate the hookworm, never wholly successful, probably did much good, but it brought no miraculous changes.[15] Then came the discovery of pellagra. Characteristically, many southern leaders, including medical men, tried at first to persuade the public that the disease did not exist, but the evidence was too strong. Notice was first taken of this disorder, already well known in Europe, in the early 1900s, but it may well have been around since long before the Civil War. It was a result of the typical diet of the impoverished southerner, too much salt pork, cornmeal, and grease, and not enough other foods. The critical shortage was of the vitamin niacin, but it would take almost a half-century to discover the cause and to arrive at a remedy.

In 1906 an outbreak of pellagra in the segregated Negro section of the Mount Vernon Insane Asylum resulted in 88 cases and 56 deaths. No doubt many of these people were suffering from the disease when admitted, because the later stages are briefly described as consisting of diarrhea, dermatitis, dementia, and death. Once pellagra was positively identified, it was found to be raging in all parts of the South. In North Carolina, which is singled out only because its records are more complete, the number of deaths from the disease increased from 273 in 1924 to 1,002 in 1930. In retrospect, many physicians wondered if perhaps pellagra had not been the cause of most of the deaths at notorious Andersonville Prison during the Civil War. Mississippi had 15,831 cases and 1,531 deaths in 1915. A rather desultory campaign to persuade the poor to keep a cow, plant a garden, and eat more beans reduced the incidence in 1916 in Mississippi to only half that of the previous year— or did the improvement come about because the price of cotton had gone up? Between the two world wars Arkansas averaged 5,000 to 10,000 cases per year with up to 500 deaths per year.

The salutary effect of the New Deal upon the diet of the South's poor is attested to by the fact that there was a steady decline in pellagra from 1933 until World War II, although the disease did not completely disappear. By the end of the war, however, commercial flour and corn meal, as well as bakery bread, were fortified with the vitamins needed to prevent pellagra and other vitamin-deficiency diseases. No amount of effort at prevention, however, can prevail completely against heartlessness on the part of men in positions of power and the abysmal ignorance among the poor. Pellagra still exists in the South, and so do other diseases associated with malnutrition.[16]

This is not to say that there has been no improvement. The South has yet a lower general health rate than the rest of the nation, but the death rate is only slightly higher. But even in today's South, where most of the impoverished are black, a black baby is twice as likely as a white baby to die within his first year.[17] When he wrote the following, Robert Coles was speaking of poor children of South Carolina's coastal counties, but he had seen the same in the Mississippi Delta and in Appalachia.

Then from the day they're born they know trouble, the kind of trouble I once would never have dreamed existed in this country. Their mothers are poorly nourished. If they have a good milk flow, that's lucky; but you don't see [baby] bottles here or many bottles of milk in these homes. The infant gets sick and there's no one to see him, no hospital for him to visit, no doctor or nurse. Pretty soon the baby becomes hungry, then undernourished. His body doesn't have enough protein, or vitamins or minerals. His bones don't develop as they should. His muscles become weak and flabby. His joints are swollen. His skin is covered with sores and infections. He may get a cold—and die, die in a matter of hours; or they live on, but with all kinds of things wrong with them. . . . We saw many of these children, and we saw the things wrong with them. We saw the food they eat; old stale bread and grits and more grits and gravy over the grits. Dr. —— claims that every day he sees diseases like rickets, scurvy, beriberi, and pellagra.[18]

Such people as these do not have a "way of life" in the usual sense of the term. Theirs is more nearly a struggle for life. They drink, at least the men do, when they have a chance, but there is little money for whiskey or even for cheap wine. They do little visiting, although social workers do sometimes complain that they will spend money that should go for food on gasoline and tires for an old car. But one thing is heartening to a southerner who has been around for a long time. As miserable as these people may be, there are not nearly so many of them as there were forty years ago. And there is another heartening fact: many families who were in that condition forty years ago are now as well off as their neighbors. In some cases they have done better than those who called them trash, black or white. Perhaps in another forty years no southerners will live in abject and degrading poverty.

11

The Winds of Change
THE CONTEMPORARY SOUTH

The South of 1980 is a far different region from the South of even one generation earlier. To analyze all the changes that have taken place is far beyond the bounds of this study, but some of the salient differences may be noted. Urbanization is the most notable change. As late as 1920, only nine cities in the South had more than 100,000 people; the decennial census of 1980 will almost certainly show as many or more with more than 1,000,000 people in their metropolitan areas. Even so, it must be remembered that the vast majority of the adults in these huge cities are of rural birth or were reared by parents who were of rural birth. Urban life forces change upon southern people, but rural habits resist change; thus southern foods have tended to remain distinctive even though every day brings additional capitulations to the standardization that afflicts all American life.[1]

The automobile has done its share to accelerate standardization. From the day of the T-Model down to that of the mass-produced T-bird, southerners have taken advantage of the mobility afforded by the automobile to see the rest of the South and of the United States. Increased wealth, two world wars, intervention in Asia, and the stationing of American troops in foreign lands have taken southerners not only to the far corners of North America but also to every other continent. I, who had seldom if ever eaten a non-traditional dish as I grew up, was taken by World War II to California, Arizona, and New Mexico in the nonsouthern states, to the Caribbean, Brazil, central and North Africa, India, Burma, and western China. In army mess halls I got American, not southern, food, and when I could I sampled the "native" dishes of the places where I found myself stationed. I was one of millions of southerners who have had the same experience over the last forty years. Thus southerners have become aware of the customs of the rest of the nation and the rest of the world, and these customs include eating habits.

While southerners who traveled became accustomed to new foods that they found outside the South, the southerner who remained at home also became more and more acquainted with alien dishes. Southerners of earlier generations might have eaten oysters even though they lived far inland, but shrimp were so unusual for those living far from salt water that they play a role as an exotic food in two of William Faulkner's novels. Yet today it is a rare southern cookbook, whether from Charleston or New Orleans or any one of scores of cities of the interior South, that does not have a recipe, and sometimes several recipes, for shrimp creole. Also, if one based his conclusion on cookbooks, he might well decide that beef Stroganoff was a traditional southern dish. The automobile, radio, television, and voluntary and involuntary travel have increasingly forced the South into the dietary mold of the rest of the nation.[2]

Another important change has been brought about by the emigration of the southern poor. Many of them, of course, migrated to southern cities, but far more, white and black, went north and west. These were the people who, during the long famine from the end of the Civil War until World War II, lived on cornmeal, biscuits, fatback, and molasses. Most of them found work wherever they went, but millions remained on the edge of starvation until added to the welfare rolls of the cities where they settled. But even on welfare they ate better than they had eaten on the land. Their migration certainly improved the southern diet; with most of the poorest gone (certainly not all) the *average* southern man or woman ate far better than his or her grandparents had.

The modern southern family may lack the self-sufficiency that a well-stocked smokehouse gave, but within reason it can choose between ham, poultry, beef, fish, preserved meats, and even lamb chops when groceries are purchased. Today's southern family does not have a garden, but it can choose between vegetables and fruits from California, Florida, the Rio Grande Valley, and the Pacific Northwest of a variety and quality that previous generations, however well off they may have been, never knew. Perhaps more important, the modern southerner has some knowledge of nutrition. This may range from an expertise close to if not matching that of a dietician to a vague realization that too much fat is bad, that every diet should include some green vegetables, and that fruit and fruit juices are healthful. Even those who know very little about nutrition are at least free from many of the erroneous notions that misled their ancestors. Despite pockets of poverty, modern southerners are the best-fed generation to live in the region since the beginning of time.[3] Compared to their Confederate or slave great-grandparents, the young people of the modern South are a generation of giants. Even the unfortunate people on the welfare rolls, using food stamps to stretch their meager incomes, are far better fed than the sharecroppers and farm laborers of the nineteenth and early twentieth centuries, and better fed, too, than many yeoman farmers of the same years.

Contributing to the quality of modern nutrition is the relative ease of preparing meals. It is fashionable to laugh at the gadgets found in modern kitchens, and some of them no doubt are status symbols more than real conveniences. But reflect upon the pressure cooker. Not only does it make the preserving of foods for future use much simpler and safer, it makes it possible for the modern southern cook to prepare in minutes cabbage, greens, broccoli, and other leafy vegetables that are unchallengeably superior to the leafy vegetables and fat meat that boiled for hours over the fireplaces or on the wood-burning stoves of fifty years ago. Consider the gas or electric stove; one turns a valve or a switch, and cooking can begin almost immediately. Compare this to the process of cutting down a tree, splitting it into stove wood, transporting the wood to the rick in the yard, carrying it into the house, starting a fire with paper and kindling, and finally adding the wood. The fire could be started faster with kerosene, but one risked singed eyebrows, and sometimes there were severe burns. And even after the fire was started, the cook had to wait thirty minutes before cooking could begin.

Consider the electric refrigerator, in which butter does not become rancid for days and milk does not sour, which provides ice cubes for iced tea or something more potent. And finally consider the deep freeze, which almost does away with the seasons insofar as foods are concerned. My own presently contains (it is April at this writing) beef roasts, crowder peas bought and shelled last July, shrimp caught last September, probably some fish from last summer though it is time to be adding more, quail presented by a friend, doves, wild ducks, and one goose shot by me, and leftovers from former meals, which, thawed and heated, will be as good as ever when put on the table. These are truly conveniences, labor-saving devices in every sense of the words, and it is a poor creature who cannot prepare a better meal with them than without them.

Of course this better diet exacts a price. There tends to be a sameness about modern foods that did not exist earlier. Fifty years ago anyone with functioning taste buds could with the first bite tell the difference between a range hog and a corn-fattened hog. It was just as easy to tell the difference between grass-fed and feeder-lot beef, though southerners tasted little enough beef from the feeder lots. One learned all too soon when a milch cow had been grazing on wild onions or bitter weed. The big "broilers" of today's supermarket, fattened in cages on carefully calculated feeds, are much blander than the considerably smaller fryers of long ago that had scratched a hard living from field and yard, getting perhaps enough corn or commercial feed to keep them scratching. But the modern broiler provides much more meat, and it is inexpensive enough that the average southerner can have fried chicken twice or more a week if he wants to. That is prosperity!

If there is good to be said for mass-production meat and vegetables, it is much harder to speak well of the "fast foods" that seem to become a bigger part of the American diet with the passing of each year. The hamburger emporiums, offering various pieces of rather

fat fried ground beef that, if not tasteless, tastes bad, are everywhere. So are oddly shaped little shops that purvey various frozen
custards which resemble, but are not, ice cream. Perhaps most
abundant of all are places serving various brands of fried chicken,
but there are fried fish shops, and one can even find establishments offering fish and chips more or less on the English model.

Tens of millions of southerners eat these fast foods regularly. Apparently they are nutritious enough, at least as far as they go, but
most of them are an insult to any palate accustomed to traditional
southern foods or, for that matter, to any good foods. People who
are still fortunate enough to live in the country, people who could
plant gardens, keep chickens, and perhaps even grow their own
beef and pork, drive into the nearest town to partake of these
abominable viands. If it were only young people too immature to
know better, it could be better borne, but whole families, even
three generations, sit in automobiles and eat abominations. And
when such families do not go to these dens of bad taste for a meal,
they nonetheless dull their appetites with carbonated drinks and
various fried and packaged items such as potato chips, cheese flavored bits of bread, and even pig skins. At least sometimes, while
the children swig soft drinks, the parents wash down the horrors
with beer.

All this should not be taken to indicate that the southern tradition in food has disappeared. On the contrary, survivals are evident
on every hand. The very fact that fried chicken is the most popular
fast food is evidence of the survival of southern tastes. Standing
alongside the hamburger palaces, especially in the upper South,
are little restaurants that still offer "all the catfish you can eat" at a
reasonable price. And that old favorite of southerners, barbecue, is
still to be had, though it ranges in quality from fit for the gods to
not fit for a dog, and one should be careful where he buys it. Ham
also remains a favorite southern dish, though most people have
lost their taste for the salty and highly seasoned country-cured
ham; they prefer the semicooked produce of a midwestern packer.
The fact that country hams are so expensive probably enters into
this preference.

Southerners still use more cornmeal and eat more corn bread than people in other sections of the nation, and biscuits frequently accompany breakfast as well as other meals, though too often they are made from a "ready mix" in a box, or even taken out of a can and baked. In those parts of the South where grits have been a standard food for more than four generations, they still hold their place. Cowpeas, especially blackeyes and crowders, remain favorites, and southerners are still big consumers of turnip greens, butter beans, watermelons, and to some extent collards. The soul food craze of some years ago, of which Aretha Franklin said, "It'll make you limber; it'll make you quick," was primarily a revival of traditional southern foods.[4] Not only have traditional southern foods survived, or at least the best of them, but dishes peculiar to regions within the South still thrive. Texas still prides itself on barbecue and chili, Kentuckians still make burgoo, and south of the Kentucky line Brunswick stew is a favorite. Virginia and North Carolina still produce superb hams; South Carolina and Georgia still use leftover rice for delicious rice puddings. Spanish bean soup and eggs Malaguena are still favorites in Florida. I have had the good fortune to live most of my adult life in south Louisiana, where boiled crayfish, turtle sauce piquante, and gumbos hold forth among many other good things.

Nor has the southern taste for game disappeared, though the press of population and improved farming methods have reduced the numbers of rabbit and quail that once were of real economic importance. But southerners still hunt rabbit and quail, and they gratefully eat them. The number of deer in the South today far exceeds the number fifty years ago, but venison will never again be eaten as widely as it was before the Civil War. Raccoon and possum are still hunted and eaten; if some method could be devised for taking the urban members of these species, they could supply many a meal. And the man fortunate enough to be able to eat waterfowl several times a year is indeed blessed.

The almost universal use of spirits, at least by men, which characterized the frontier and antebellum South came to an end in the years after the Civil War, and the South is still the heir of Protestant prohibitionism. In a survey taken in the late 1960s, two-thirds of the southern Protesants questioned stated that they were teetotalers, and almost half of them favored the restoration of national prohibition. Some of these people, of course, "vote dry as long as they can stagger to the polls," but most of them are sincere. The rural and small-town southerners, and probably most urban southerners, if they drink at all, do so on the sly, probably facing the disapproval of wives and families. Indeed, since by taking a drink he has already sinned almost beyond redemption, the southerner frequently goes on to get roaring drunk. Since so much of the South is legally dry through the workings of local option, the drinker is just as likely to drink rather bad moonshine as to drink some cheap brand with tax stamps on it.

On the other hand, the modern South does have "a burgeoning new middle class, laden with the largess of an affluent society," which is able to "indulge expensive and exotic tastes in food and clothes and liquor."[5] The cocktail party has become as much of a social institution in the South as elsewhere in the nation. Observation indicates that most southerners, male and female, drink bourbon and water at such affairs, but there are those who indulge in strange mixtures. For a society as conservative as that of the South, the modern cocktail party does represent a rather radical change. A generation ago professional men, especially educators, still lowered their shades before they brought out a bottle in their own homes. Today, often in defiance of law, public colleges and universities permit, and sometimes finance, cocktail parties; sometimes, even, they are held on campus. Nor are people shocked, as one lady of my acquaintance once was, to see a Protestant clergyman "dangling his cross in his cocktail."

For good or ill, southerners have learned much about drinking in the past thirty years. Shortly after World War II, a regional scholarly association, meeting in an old and gracious southern city, was for all practical purposes disabled for a day by a particularly delicious and virulently potent punch; famous men disgraced themselves in the hotel lobby. Recently I attended a meeting of educators where the same punch was the only alcoholic beverage, and if anyone took too much, he concealed it well.

The cocktail party has in a sense replaced the "groaning board" of the great plantation of the Old South as an occasion for filling one's guests with the best of food. The parties given by businesses are usually the most opulent, obviously because the cost is tax deductible. At a convention in New Orleans recently, publishers set forth for their guests fried shrimp, fried catfish, oysters Rockefeller, crab meat, ham, roast beef, many kinds of cheese, olives, nuts, fresh strawberries, and good wines, plus the usual whiskey, gin, vodka, and rum. But at a private home in a small city I have seen roast beef, ham, shrimp both fried and boiled, crayfish etouffe, fried oysters, Swedish meatballs, venison, roasted alligator tail, anchovies, smoked wild duck, cheeses, nuts, olives, and various pickles provided for dozens of guests. A Virginia Carter or a South Carolina Middleton could have offered no more, though presumably there would have been fewer guests, and they would not have eaten on their feet.

The modern South shares with the rest of the United States the recent fascination with table wines. Few southerners have acquired really expert tastes, but many of them are trying. Wine, however, is a middle- or upper-middle-class drink. The "good ole boy" (or girl) drinks beer. At baseball games, stock car races, rodeos, and even New Orleans' Mardi Gras, prodigious quantities of beer are consumed. American beer, basically German in origin, has little resemblance to that of England, but the South has at least returned to the beer-drinking tradition of the Elizabethans. For what it may be worth, Louisianians of French ancestry are among the most inveterate beer drinkers of all.

Southern hospitality still exists, but it has changed. It is more likely to be expressed in the cocktail party or "coffee" than in the extended visit of yesteryear. In fact, the modern house is poorly adapted to the month-long visits which were not uncommon even fifty years ago. At the same time, however, the automobile and good roads have made "spending the day" far simpler; there is no real need for long visits except when people live great distances apart. Also, the so-called extended family seems to be rapidly disappearing. Probably there were closer emotional ties between cousins in the older rural South than there are between brothers in the urban South of today. The telephone provides a substitute for much of the visiting that once was almost routine. When today's southerner says "Y'all come," he is simply being polite unless he adds a specific day and time. If he does, it may be an invitation.

Notes

Chapter 1

1. Thomas Perkins Abernethy, *Three Virginia Frontiers* (Baton Rouge: Louisiana State University Press, 1940), 45–46.

2. *Ibid.*, 6–7; Carl Bridenbaugh, *Myths and Realities: Societies of the Colonial South* (Baton Rouge: Louisiana State University Press, 1952), 114, 133–35.

3. Richard A. Bartlett, *The New Country: A Social History of the American Frontier* (New York: Oxford University Press, 1974), 118.

4. "Some Particulars Relative to the Soil, Situation, Production, &c of Kentucky: Extracted from the Manuscript Journal of a Gentlemen Not Long Since Returned from Those Parts," *National Gazette*, I (November, 1791), 1–3, rpr. Eugene L. Schwaab (ed.), *Travels in the Old South, Selected from Periodicals of the Time* (Lexington: University Press of Kentucky, 1973), I, 60. See also Thomas D. Clark, *Frontier America: The Story of the Western Movement* (New York: Charles Scribner's Sons, 1959), 202; William Byrd III, "Secret History of the Dividing Line," in Louis B. Wright (ed.), *The Prose Works of William Byrd of Westover: Narratives of a Colonial Virginian* (Cambridge, Mass.: Belknap Press of Harvard University Press, 1966), 140; Everett Dick, *The Dixie Frontier: A Social History of the Southern Frontier from the First Transmontane Beginnings to the Civil War* (New York: Capricorn Books, 1964), 287.

5. Dick, *Dixie Frontier*, 288.

6. Gertrude I. Thomas, *Foods of Our Forefathers* (Philadelphia: F. A. Davis, 1941), 63; Reginald Horsman, *The Frontier in the Formative Years, 1783–1815* (New York: Holt, Rinehart and Winston, 1970), 115; Byrd, "Secret History of the Dividing Line," in Wright (ed.), *Prose Works of William Byrd*, 117.

7. William Byrd III, "History of the Dividing Line," in Wright (ed.), *Prose Works of William Byrd*, 232; Harriette Arnow, *Flowering of the Cumberland* (New York: Macmillan, 1963), 355; quoted in Thomas D. Clark, *The Rampaging Frontier: Manners and Humor of Pioneer Days in the South and the Middle West* (Indianapolis: Bobbs-Merrill, 1939), 148.

8. Byrd, "Secret History of the Dividing Line," in Wright (ed.), *Prose Works of William Byrd*, 103; Dick, *Dixie Frontier*, 33–34, 287; Ray Tannehill, *Food in History* (New York: Stein and Day, 1973), 266–67.

9. Brown Wiggins interview, in Campbell Loughmiller and Lynn Loughmiller (eds.), *Big Thicket Legacy* (Austin: University of Texas Press, 1977), 21; Dick, *Dixie Frontier*, 107.

10. Byrd, "Secret History of the Dividing Line," in Wright (ed.), *Prose Works of*

William Byrd, 113–14; Dick, *Dixie Frontier*, 35, 287; Horsman, *The Frontier in the Formative Years*, 116.

11. Byrd, "History of the Dividing Line," in Wright (ed.), *Prose Works of William Byrd*, 234; George Henry Preble, "The Diary of a Canoe Expedition into the Everglades and Interior of Southern Florida in 1842," *United Service*, VIII (April, 1883), 358–78, rpr. Schwaab (ed.), *Travels in the Old South*, 371–77; Dick, *Dixie Frontier*, 287–88.

12. Harnett T. Kane, *The Southern Christmas Book: The Full Story from the Earliest Times to the Present: People, Customs, Conviviality, Carols, Cooking* (New York: D. McKay, 1958), 241.

13. Dick, *Dixie Frontier*, 291.

14. Ray Allen Billington and James Blaine Hedges, *Westward Expansion: A History of the American Frontier* (New York: Macmillan, 1960), 47.

15. Horsman. *The Frontier in the Formative Years*, 116; Sam Bowers Hilliard, *Hog Meat and Hoecake: Food Supply in the Old South* (Carbondale: Southern Illinois University Press, 1972), 39–40.

16. Quoted in Rupert B. Vance, *Human Geography of the South* (Chapel Hill: University of North Carolina Press, 1935), 415–16.

17. Dick, *Dixie Frontier*, 289–90; Tannehill, *Food in History*, 265.

18. Thomas, *Foods of Our Fathers*, 41.

19. Tannehill, *Food in History*, 295.

20. Arnow, *Flowering of the Cumberland*, 272–73, 277–79; Ray Allen Billington, *America's Frontier Heritage* (New York: Holt, Rinehart and Winston, 1966), 71; Bridenbaugh, *Myths and Realities*, 177–78; Dick, *Dixie Frontier*, 292.

21. Quoted in Bridenbaugh, *Myths and Realities*, 174. See also Arnow, *Flowering of the Cumberland*, 280.

22. Billington, *America's Frontier Heritage*, 214–15; Dick, *Dixie Frontier*, 324.

23. Arnow, *Flowering of the Cumberland*, 329–30; Francis Harper (ed.), *Travels of William Bartram* (New Haven: Yale University Press, 1958), 23, *passim*; Bartlett, *The New Country*, 147.

Chapter 2

1. Frank Lawrence Owsley, *Plain Folk of the Old South* (Baton Rouge: Louisiana State University Press, 1949), 72; Frank Lawrence Owsley, "The Pattern of Migration and Settlement on the Southern Frontier," in Harriette Chappell Owsley (ed.), *The South: Old and New Frontiers* (Athens: University of Georgia Press, 1969), 9; Loughmiller and Loughmiller (eds.), *Big Thicket Legacy, passim*.

2. Benjamin Albert Botkin (ed.), *A Treasury of Southern Folklore: Stories, Ballads, Traditions, and Folkways of the People of the South* (New York: Crown, 1949), 550.

3. Thomas, *Foods of Our Forefathers*, 62; Charles H. Sherrill, *French Memories of Eighteenth-Century America* (New York: Charles Scribner's Sons, 1915), 80–81.

4. Mary Jones to Charles C. Jones, Jr., April 22, 1856, in Robert Manson Myers (ed.), *The Children of Pride: A True Story of Georgia and the Civil War* (New Haven: Yale University Press, 1972), 210.

5. Clark, *Frontier America*, 212; Julia Cherry Spruill, *Women's Life and Work in the Southern Colonies* (New York: Russell and Russell, 1969), 25–29.

6. Spruill, *Women's Life and Work*, 25.

7. *Ibid.*, 68–69, 187; George C. Rogers, Jr., *Charleston in the Age of the Pinck-*

neys (Norman: University of Oklahoma Press, 1969), 79–80; Susan Dabney Smedes, *Memorials of a Southern Planter* (Baltimore: Cushings and Bailey, 1888), 33; Katherine M. Jones (ed.), *The Plantation South* (Indianapolis: Bobbs-Merrill, 1957), 61; Mary Jones Mallard to Mary Taylor Jones, August 12, 1857, in Myers (ed.), *Children of Pride*, 364.

8. Quoted in Bridenbaugh, *Myths and Realities*, 172–73; James Pearse, *A Narrative of the Life of James Pearse* (Chicago: Quadrangle Books, 1962), 61–62; Dolores Egger Labbe, "Women in Early Nineteenth-Century Louisiana" (Ph.D. dissertation, University of Delaware, 1975), 162.

9. Jonathan Daniels, *A Southerner Discovers the South* (New York: Macmillan, 1938), 253; Dick, *Dixie Frontier*, 289–90; Hilliard, *Hog Meat and Hoecake*, 38, 48–49; Thomas, *Foods of Our Forefathers*, 43.

10. Hilliard, *Hog Meat and Hoecake*, 8, 31; Clark, *Frontier America*, 215; Vance, *Human Geography of the South*, 417.

11. Hilliard, *Hog Meat and Hoecake*, 8; Joseph G. Baldwin, *The Flush Times of Alabama and Mississippi: A Series of Sketches* (New York: Sagamore Press, 1957), 37, 104; Mary Jones to Mary Sharpe Jones, January 2, 1857, in Myers (ed.), *Children of Pride*, 290.

12. Byrd, "Secret History of the Dividing Line," in Wright (ed.), *The Prose Works of William Byrd*, 59.

13. Quoted in Hilliard, *Hog Meat and Hoecake*, 42; quoted in Sherrill, *French Memories*, 80–81.

14. Hilliard, *Hog Meat and Hoecake*, 9, 100; Vance, *Human Geography of the South*, 416; Dick, *Dixie Frontier*, 35–36.

15. Quoted in Arnow, *Flowering of the Cumberland*, 222. See also Hilliard, *Hog Meat and Hoecake*, 95–96, 101.

16. Hilliard, *Hog Meat and Hoecake*, 95–98, 101.

17. Laura E. Maxwell to Mary Jones, March 11, 1855, in Myers (ed.), *Children of Pride*, 142; Hilliard, *Hog Meat and Hoecake*, 44.

18. Hilliard, *Hog Meat and Hoecake*, 43; Dick, *Dixie Frontier*, 288; Alfred Leland Crabb, *Nashville: Personality of a City* (Indianapolis: Bobbs-Merrill, 1960), 105.

19. Hilliard, *Hog Meat and Hoecake*, 43–44.

20. *Ibid.*, 41; the Reverend C.C. Jones to Charles C. Jones, Jr., November 30, 1856, in Myers (ed.), *Children of Pride*, 269; Spruill, *Women's Life and Work*, 82; Crabb, *Nashville*, 102; Arnow, *Flowering of the Cumberland*, 221.

21. Hilliard, *Hog Meat and Hoecake*, 9, 40, 112–13.

22. *Ibid.*, 129–30.

23. *Ibid.*, 44–45, 129–30.

24. *Ibid.*, 45; Amos Andrew Parker, *A Trip to the West and Texas* (New York: Arno Press, 1973), 123, 148; Labbe, "Women in Louisiana," 90; Charles C. Jones, Jr., to Mary Jones, May 25, 1859, Mary Jones to Charles C. Jones, Jr., August 16, 1859, in Myers (ed.), *Children of Pride*, 486, 506.

25. Hilliard, *Hog Meat and Hoecake*, 45–46, 143; Clark, *Frontier America*, 218; Smedes, *Memorials of a Southern Planter*, 82; J.S. Buckingham, *The Slave States of America* (New York: Negro Universities Press, 1968), II, 159–60; Mary S. Mallard to Mary Jones, May 29, 1860, Rev. C.C. Jones to Susan M. Cummings, June 30, 1860, in Myers (ed.), *Children of Pride*, 582, 589, *passim.*

26. Arnow, *Flowering of the Cumberland*, 215–18; Hilliard, *Hog Meat and Hoecake*, 131–32; Mary S. Mallard to Laura E. Buttolph, June 24, 1858, Mary S. Mallard to Louisa J. Robarts, April 30, 1859, in Myers (ed.), *Children of Pride*, 425, 478; *The Wise Encyclopedia of Cooking* (New York: H. M. Wise, 1952), 629.

27. Hilliard, *Hog Meat and Hoecake*, 46–47, 146–48; Thomas, *Foods of Our Forefathers*, 50; Kane, *Southern Christmas*, 154.
28. Labbe, "Women in Louisiana," 160.
29. Botkin (ed.), *Treasury of Southern Folklore*, 23; Dorothea C. Cooper (ed.), *Kentucky Hospitality: A 200-Year Tradition* (Lexington: University Press of Kentucky, 1976), 186–87; Tannehill, *Food in History*, 300; Hilliard, *Hog Meat and Hoecake*, 47–48, 74–80; *The Wise Encyclopedia of Cookery*, 133–34, 139–40.
30. Hilliard, *Hog Meat and Hoecake*, 81–82.
31. *Ibid.*, 81–83; Labbe, "Women in Louisiana," 160; the Reverend C.C. Jones to Mary Jones, December 10, 1856, in Myers (ed.), *Children of Pride*, 271; Botkin (ed.), *Treasury of Southern Folklore*, 231.
32. Hilliard, *Hog Meat and Hoecake*, 85–86, 88–89; Hugh Jones, *The Present State of Virginia: From Whence Is Inferred a Short View of Maryland and North Carolina*, ed. Richard L. Morton (Chapel Hill: Published for the Virginia Historical Society by the University of North Carolina Press, 1956), 78; Mary Jones to Mary Sharpe Jones, October 9, 1855, Eliza G. Robarts to the Reverend C. C. Jones, June 2, 1856, the Reverend C. C. Jones to Charles C. Jones, Jr., March 15, 1858, July 30, 1858, in Myers (ed.), *Children of Pride*, 159, 221, 398, 433; Warren S. Tryon (ed.), *A Mirror for Americans: Life and Manners in the United States, 1790–1870, As Recorded by American Travelers* (Chicago: University of Chicago Press, 1952), II, 259; William Howard Russell, *My Diary North and South*, ed. Fletcher Pratt (New York: Harper and Brothers, 1954), 108, 131.
33. Hilliard, *Hog Meat and Hoecake*, 88–89.

Chapter 3

1. Hilliard, *Hog Meat and Hoecake*, 48–50; Dick, *Dixie Frontier*, 290; Botkin, *Treasury of Southern Folklore*, 568; Frederick Law Olmsted, *A Journey in the Seaboard Slave States* (New York: Negro Universities Press, 1856), 476–77; Thomas, *Foods of Our Forefathers*, 50.
2. Dick, *Dixie Frontier*, 289–91; Crabb, *Nashville*, 111; Parker, *Trip to the West and Texas*, 108; Hilliard, *Hog Meat and Hoecake*, 178–79.
3. Owsley, "Pattern of Migration," 9–10.
4. Hilliard, *Hog Meat and Hoecake*, 50, 175; Dick, *Dixie Frontier*, 290–91; Bernard Romans, *A Concise Natural History of East and West Florida* (New Orleans: Pelican, 1961), 86; Mary Jones to Charles C. Jones, Jr., September 26, 1859, in Myers (ed.), *Children of Pride*, 520–21.
5. Hilliard, *Hog Meat and Hoecake*, 173, 177; Romans, *Concise Natural History*, 86.
6. Thomas, *Foods of Our Forefathers*, 50; Hilliard, *Hog Meat and Hoecake*, 50, 173–75; Arnow, *Flowering of the Cumberland*, 361; Sherrill, *French Memories*, 104.
7. A. Krapovickas, "The Origin, Variability and Spread of the Groundnut," in Peter J. Vucko and G. W. Dimbleby (eds.), *The Domestication and Exploitation of Plants and Animals* (Chicago: Aldine, 1969), 433–37; Thomas, *Foods of Our Forefathers*, 50; Clark, *Frontier America*, 215; Tryon (ed.), *Mirror for Americans*, II, 245; Charles B. Heiser, *Nightshades: The Paradoxical Plants* (San Francisco: W. H. Freeman, 1969), 9, 13, 49, 57; Barbara Black, "Food Plants America Gave the World," *Horticulture*, XLVIII (July, 1970), 24–26ff.; Thomas Jefferson, *Notes on the State of Virginia* (New York: Harper and Row, 1964), 37; Romans, (*Concise Natural History*, 91; Hilliard, *Hog Meat and Hoecake*, 172–74.

8. Jefferson, *Notes on Virginia*, 37; Spruill, *Women's Life and Work*, 67–68; Moreau de Saint Mery, *Voyage aux Etats-Unis de L'Amerique, 1793–1798*, ed. Stewart L. Mims (New Haven: Yale University Press, 1913), 62–63; Clark, *Frontier America*, 215; Hilliard, *Hog Meat and Hoecake*, 172–75.

9. Tryon (ed.), *Mirror for Americans*, II, 286; Olmsted, *Journey in the Seaboard Slave States*, 414; Guion Griffis Johnson, *Ante-Bellum North Carolina: A Social History* (Chapel Hill: University of North Carolina Press, 1937), 137–39; Pearse, *Narrative of the Life of James Pearse*, 60.

10. Tryon (ed.), *Mirror for Americans*, II, 285–86; Charles C. Jones, Jr., to Mary Jones, July 12, 1856, in Myers (ed.), *Children of Pride*, 227; Gloria Jahoda, *Florida: A Bicentennial History* (New York: W. W. Norton, 1976), 103–108.

11. Hilliard, *Hog Meat and Hoecake*, 50–51, 90, 181; Jones, *Present State of Virginia*, 78; John Melish, *Travels Through the United States of America in the Years 1806 and 1807, and 1809, 1810, and 1811: Including an Account of Passages Betwixt America and Britain, and Travels Through Various Parts of Britain, Ireland, and Canada, with Corrections and Improvements Till 1815* (New York: Johnson Reprint, 1970), 108.

12. Hilliard, *Hog Meat and Hoecake*, 50–51, 90.

13. *Ibid.*, 50–51. Dick, *Dixie Frontier*, 291; Byrd, "Secret History of the Dividing Line," in Wright (ed.), *Prose Works of William Byrd*, 66; Tryon (ed.), *Mirror for Americans*, II, 267; Labbe, "Women in Louisiana," 82.

14. Hilliard, *Hog Meat and Hoecake*, 40–41.

15. Byrd, "Secret History of the Dividing Line," in Wright (ed.), *Prose Works of William Byrd*, 64; Hilliard, *Hog Meat and Hoecake*, 52; Frances Trollope, "Cooking, Amusements and Money Getting," in Allan Nevins (ed.), *America Through British Eyes* (New York: Oxford University Press, 1948), 134.

16. Harper (ed.), *Travels of William Bartram*, 196.

17. Sherrill, *French Memories*, 81–82; Harold E. Davis, *The Fledgeling Province: Social and Cultural Life in Colonial Georgia* (Chapel Hill: Published for the Institute of Early American History and Culture by the University of North Carolina Press, 1976), 72–73.

18. Buckingham, *Slave States of America*, I, 125, II, 329; Byrd, "Secret History of the Dividing Line" and "History of the Dividing Line," in Wright (ed.), *Prose Works of William Byrd*, 65, 215; Davis, *Fledgling Province*, 73; Johnson, *Ante-Bellum North Carolina*, 159–60; Jones, *Present State of Virginia*, 86, 91, 138; John Melish, "Celebrating the Fourth at Louisville, Georgia," in Nevins (ed.), *America Through British Eyes*, 49.

19. Byrd, "History of the Dividing Line," in Wright (ed.), *Prose Works of William Byrd*, 205; Davis, *Fledgeling Province*, 75; Tannehill, *Food in History*, 298; Tryon (ed.), *Mirror for Americans*, II, 257; Sherrill, *French Memories*, 79–80; Isaac Weld, Jr., *Travels Through the States of North America and the Provinces of Upper and Lower Canada During the Years 1795, 1796 & 1797* (New York: A. M. Kelley, 1970), 182.

20. Arnow, *Flowering of the Cumberland*, 297–80, 408; Billington, *Frontier Heritage*, 96; Buckingham, *Slave States of America*, II, 17–18; Johnson, *Ante-Bellum North Carolina*, 142–43.

21. Johnson, *Ante-Bellum North Carolina*, 95–97, 142–43, 152–53; Tryon (ed.), *Mirror for Americans*, II, 266; Bridenbaugh, *Myths and Realities*, 23.

22. Johnson, *Ante-Bellum North Carolina*, 169; Hilliard, *Hog Meat and Hoecake*, 52; Labbe, "Women in Louisiana," 45–46.

23. Davis, *Fledgling Province*, 61–62; George Wilson Pierson, *Toqueville in America* (Garden City, N.Y.: Anchor Books, 1959), 372; Jones (ed.), *Plantation*

South, 309; Parker, *Trip to the West and Texas*, 93, *passim*; Frederick Law Olmsted, *Journey in the Back Country* (New York: Schocken Books, 1972), *passim*.

24. Buckingham, *Slave States of America*, I, 124, 225, II, 148–49, 257–58; Harriet Martineau, *Society in America* (Garden City, N.Y.: Anchor Books, 1962), 157; John Stevens Cabot Abbott, *South and North, or Impressions Received During a Trip to Cuba and the South* (New York: Negro Universities Press, 1969), 112.

25. Tryon (ed.), *Mirror for Americans*, II, 246; Arnow, *Flowering of the Cumberland*, 141–42, 408–409; Davis, *Fledgeling Province*, 61; Hilliard, *Hog Meat and Hoecake*, 54–55.

26. Labbe, "Women in Louisiana," 56–57.

27. Spruill, *Women's Life and Work*, 86–87, 110–11; Labbe, "Women in Louisiana," 56–57; Dick, *Dixie Frontier*, 135–37, 236–37; Clark, *Rampaging Frontier*, 262–63, 269–70; 283; Jones (ed.), *The Plantation South*, 270.

28. Johnson, *Ante-Bellum North Carolina*, 146; Dick, *Dixie Frontier*, 222–24; Labbe, "Women in Louisiana," 56; Spruill, *Women's Life and Work*, 86–87.

29. Dick, *Dixie Frontier*, 125–27; Clark, *Rampaging Frontier*, 267–68; Tannehill, *Food in History*, 265–66; Smedes, *Memorials of a Southern Planter*, 67.

30. Dick, *Dixie Frontier*, 127–37; Clark, *Rampaging Frontier*, 266; Johnson, *Ante-Bellum North Carolina*, 91–92.

31. Labbe, "Women in Louisiana," 148–50; Tryon (ed.), *Mirror for Americans*, II, 242, 401; Buckingham, *Slave States of America*, II, 391–92; Johnson, *Ante-Bellum North Carolina*, 156–57. 160–61.

Chapter 4

1. Jones (ed.), *The Plantation South*, 5, 7; Spruill, *Women's Life and Work*, 24–25, 37; Howard W. Odum, *American Epoch: Southern Portraiture in the National Picture* (New York: H. Holt, 1930), 35.

2. Jones (ed.), *The Plantation South*, 48, 81, 88, 218; Bridenbaugh, *Myths and Realities*, 69–70, 72; Anne Firor Scott, *The Southern Lady: From Pedestal to Politics, 1830-1930* (Chicago: University of Chicago Press, 1970), 33.

3. Quoted in Jones (ed.), *The Plantation South*, 125; *ibid.*, 151, 174; Crabb, *Nashville*, 118.

4. Russell, *Diary North and South*, 143, 148; Smedes, *Memorials of a Southern Planter*, 59-60; Mary Jones to Charles C. Jones, Jr., October 2, 1856, in Myers (ed.), *Children of Pride*, 245.

5. Quoted in Dixon Wecter, *The Saga of American Society: A Record of Social Aspiration, 1607–1937* (New York: Charles Scribner's Sons, 1937), 25–26.

6. Quoted in Tryon (ed.), *Mirror for Americans*, II, 260; Olmsted, *Journey in the Seaboard Slave States*, 80, 92.

7. Quoted in Hilliard, *Hog Meat and Hoecake*, 54; Wecter, *Saga of Society*, 33.

8. Quoted in Hilliard, *Hog Meat and Hoecake*, 54.

9. Crabb, *Nashville*, 119; Myers (ed.), *Children of Pride*, *passim*; Jones (ed.), *The Plantation South*, 328–29.

10. Martineau, *Society in America*, 156.

11. Quoted in Jones (ed.), *The Plantation South*, 49; Smedes, *Memorials of a Southern Planter*, 81.

12. Wecter, *Saga of Society*, 26; Jones (ed.), *The Plantation South*, 7, 109; Martineau, *Society in America*, 156.

13. Smedes, *Memorials of a Southern Planter*, 160; Kane, *Southern Christmas*,

10–11; Jones (ed.), *The Plantation South*, 83, 130; Robert Carter to Edward Tucker, July 13, 1720, Carter to James Arbuckle, July 18, 1720, in Louis B. Wright (ed.), *Letters of Robert Carter, 1720–1727; The Commercial Interests of a Virginia Gentleman* (Westport, Conn.: Greenwood Press, 1970), 15–16, 30–31; Sherrill, *French Memories*, 78–79.

14. Russell, *Diary North and South*, 149; Sherrill, *French Memories*, 78–79; Jones (ed.), *The Plantation South*, 228–30, 338.

15. Harper (ed.), *Travels of William Bartram*, 7; Sherrill, *French Memories*, 74–76; Rogers, *Charleston*, 82–83.

16. Quoted in Jones (ed.), *The Plantation South*, 157, 32, 166.

17. The Reverend C. C. Jones to the Reverend and Mrs. R.Q. Mallard, June 12, 1857, in Myers (ed.), *Children of Pride*, 327–28; Weld, *Travels Through North America*, 142–43; Johnson, *Ante-Bellum North Carolina*, 83; Jones (ed.), *The Plantation South*, 80.

18. Quoted in Jones (ed.), *The Plantation South*, 63; Spruill, *Women's Life and Work*, 94. See also Kane, *Southern Christmas*, 19. Jones (ed.), *The Plantation South*, 251.

19. Louis B. Wright and Marion Tinling (eds.), *The Secret Diary of William Byrd of Westover, 1709–1712* (Richmond: Dietz Press, 1941), 67, 72, 86; Jones (ed.), *The Plantation South*, 245–55.

20. Kane, *Southern Christmas*, 10; quoted in Jones (ed.), *The Plantation South*, 14, 241.

21. Katherine Du Pre Lumpkin, *The Making of a Southerner* (New York: Alfred A. Knopf, 1947), 39; quoted in Jones (ed.), *The Plantation South*, 67; Smedes, *Memorials of a Southern Planter*, 165–66; Wecter, *Saga of Society*, 28.

22. Quoted in Jones (ed.), *The Plantation South*, 63–64.

23. *Ibid.*; Bridenbaugh, *Myths and Realities*, 24–25; Spruill, *Women's Life and Work*, 102, 105.

24. Quoted in Jones (ed.), *The Plantation South*, 238; Wecter, *Saga of Society*, 28.

Chapter 5

1. Clark, *Rampaging Frontier*, 109; Baldwin, *Flush Times of Alabama and Mississippi*, 58, 73; Labbe, "Women in Louisiana," 100–101.

2. Spruill, *Women's Life and Work*, 41; Russell, *Diary North and South*, 158.

3. Weld, *Travels Through North America*, 236; William F. Gray, *From Virginia to Texas, 1835: Diary of Col. William F. Gray, Giving Details of His Journey to Texas and Return in 1835–1836 and Second Journey to Texas in 1837, with Preface by A. C. Gray* (Houston: Fletcher Young, 1965), 5; Martineau, *Society in America*, 275; Buckingham, *Slave States of America*, II, 293–94; Nevins (ed.), *America Through British Eyes*, 101.

4. Buckingham, *Slave States of America*, II, 285–86, 304, 365, 479; Jones (ed.), *The Plantation South*, 256.

5. Buckingham, *Slave States of America*, II, 4–5; Tryon (ed.), *Mirror for Americans*, II, 453; Johnson, *Ante-Bellum North Carolina*, 91; Melish, *Travels Through the United States*, 192.

6. Gray, *From Virginia to Texas*, 197; Buckingham, *Slave States of America*, I, 225, II, 155–56; quoted in Hilliard, *Hog Meat and Hoecake*, 39.

7. Gray, *From Virginia to Texas*, 35, 40; Tryon (ed.), *Mirror for Americans*, II, 271.

8. Labbe, "Women in Louisiana," 95–96, 133, 144; Parker, *Trip to the West and Texas*, 112; Gray, *From Virginia to Texas*, 171.

9. Quoted in Schwaab (ed.), *Travels in the Old South*, 427; Gray, *From Virginia to Texas*, 107; Parker, *Trip to the West and Texas*, *passim*; Frederick Law Olmsted, *A Journey Through Texas* (Austin: University of Texas Press, 1978), *passim*.

10. Melish, *Travels Through the United States*, 39; Weld, *Travels Through North America*, 41–42; Buckingham, *Slave States of America*, II, 172; Smedes, *Memorials of a Southern Planter*, 51–52; Charles C. Jones, Jr., to the Reverend and Mrs. C. C. Jones, July 19, 1854, in Myers (ed.), *Children of Pride*, 63; Gray, *From Virginia to Texas*, 86, 120, 164, 220; Parker, *Trip to the West and Texas*, 100, 119.

11. Quoted in Jones (ed.), *The Plantation South*, 296.

12. *Ibid.*, 308.

13. Buckingham, *Slave States of America*, I, 467–68.

14. *Ibid.*, 397–98, 468; Olmsted, *Journey in the Seaboard Slave States*, 611; Gray, *From Virginia to Texas*, 14, 16.

15. Bridenbaugh, *Myths and Realities*, 95, 179; Spruill, *Women's Life and Work*, 109; Schwaab (ed.), *Travels in the Old South*, 349; Cooper (ed.), *Kentucky Hospitality*, 36–42; Labbe, "Women in Louisiana," 155; James F. Sulzby, Jr., *Historic Alabama Hotels and Resorts* (University, Ala.: University of Alabama Press, 1960), 5–6.

16. Buckingham, *Slave States of America*, II, 194–96.

17. *Ibid.*, 306–307.

18. *Ibid.*, 315, 339, 355.

19. Quoted in Tryon (ed.), *Mirror for Americans*, II, 392–93.

20. Gray, *From Virginia to Texas*, 4; Buckingham, *Slave States of America*, II, 316–17; Schwaab (ed.), *Travels in the Old South*, 525–26; Mary Jones to Mary S. Mallard, June 26, 1857, Mary Jones to Charles C. Jones, Jr., June 30, 1857, in Myers (ed.), *Children of Pride*, 339, 342.

21. Buckingham, *Slave States of America*, I, 246, II, 149–50; Olmsted, *Journey in the Seaboard Slave States*, 548, and *Journey in the Back Country*, 126–27; Buckingham, *Slave States of America*, I, 450–51.

22. Russell, *Diary North and South*, 18–19; Nevins (ed.), *America Through British Eyes*, 141; Buckingham, *Slave States of America*, II, 574; Robert Somers, *The Southern States Since the War* (New York: Arno Press, 1973), 38; Tryon, *Mirror for Americans*, II, 399.

23. Martineau, *Society in America*, 152; Sulzby, *Alabama Hotels and Resorts*, 126; Daniels, *A Southerner Discovers the South*, 270; Abbott, *South and North*, 127; Buckingham, *Slave States of America*, I, 283.

24. Buckingham, *Slave States of America*, I, 297, 331.

25. Schwaab (ed.), *Travels in the Old South*, 349; Charles C. Jones, Jr., to the Reverend and Mrs. C. C. Jones, August 19, 1854, in Myers (ed.), *Children of Pride*, 72; Russell, *Diary North and South*, 154–55.

26. Olmsted, *Journey in the Seaboard Slave States*, 625.

27. Quoted in Stanley J. Folmsbee, Robert E. Corlew, and Enoch L. Mitchell, *Tennessee: A Short History* (Knoxville: University of Tennessee Press, 1969), 300, 301; quoted in Schwaab (ed.), *Travels in the Old South*, 349.

28. Quoted in Jones (ed.), *The Plantation South*, 207. See also Buckingham, *Slave States of America*, II, 234; Schwaab (ed.), *Travels in the Old South*, 566.

29. Mary Jones to Mary S. Mallard, August 17, 1866, in Myers (ed.), *Children of Pride*, 1349; quoted in Kane, *Southern Christmas*, 130.

Chapter 6

1. Davis, *Fledgeling Province*, 134; Eugene Genovese, *Roll, Jordan, Roll: The World the Slaves Made* (New York: Pantheon Books, 1974), 540–49; Julia Floyd Smith, *Slavery and Plantation Growth in Antebellum Florida* (Gainesville: University of Florida Press, 1973), 139; Olmsted, *Journey in the Seaboard Slave States*, 88–115; Joe Gray Taylor, *Negro Slavery in Louisiana* (Baton Rouge: Louisiana Historical Association, 1963), 100–101, 106–109; Richard C. Wade, *Slavery in the Cities: The South, 1820–1860* (New York: Oxford University Press, 1964), 132–33.

2. Norman R. Yetman (ed.), *Life Under the "Peculiar Institution": Selections from the Slave Narratives* (New York: Holt, Rinehart and Winston, 1970), 73.

3. Smedes, *Memorials of a Southern Planter*, 163; Hilliard, *Hog Meat and Hoecake*, 57–58, 107; Joe Gray Taylor, *Louisiana Reconstructed, 1863–1877* (Baton Rouge: Louisiana State University Press, 1975), 328.

4. Hilliard, *Hog Meat and Hoecake*, 58–59; the Reverend C. C. Jones to Mary Jones, November 24, 1859, in Myers (ed.), *Children of Pride*, 540; Smedes, *Memorials of a Southern Planter*, 58–59; Russell, *Diary North and South*, 143.

5. Thomas Elliott Campbell, *Colonial Caroline: A History of Caroline County, Virginia* (Richmond: Dietz Press, 1954), 334; Genovese, *Roll, Jordan, Roll*, 599–609; John Blassingame, *The Slave Community: Plantation Life in the Antebellum South* (New York: Oxford University Press, 1972), 159.

6. Solomon Northup, *Twelve Years a Slave*, ed. Sue Eakin and Joseph Logsdon (Baton Rouge: Louisiana State University Press, 1968), 153.

7. Hilliard, *Hog Meat and Hoecake*, 48; Northup, *Twelve Years a Slave*, 152–55; Theodore Rosengarten (ed.), *All God's Dangers: The Life of Nate Shaw* (New York: Alfred A. Knopf, 1974), 376–82.

8. Hilliard, *Hog Meat and Hoecake*, 61; Yetman (ed.), *Life Under the "Peculiar Institution*," 337; Jones (ed.), *The Plantation South*, 271–72.

9. Jones (ed.), *The Plantation South*, 271–72; the Reverend C. C. Jones to Susan M. Cummings, June 4, 1857, in Myers (ed.), *Children of Pride*, 322; Hilliard, *Hog Meat and Hoecake*, 39, 60, 174.

10. Hilliard, *Hog Meat and Hoecake*, 60–61; Jones (ed.), *The Plantation South*, 271–72.

11. Yetman (ed.), *Life Under the "Peculiar Institution*," 264–65.

12. Kenneth F. Kiple and Virginia H. Kiple, "Slave Child Mortality: Some Nutritional Answers to a Perennial Puzzle," *Journal of Southern History*, X (1977), 284–309; Todd L. Savitt, *Medicine and Slavery: The Diseases and Care of Blacks in Antebellum Virginia* (Urbana: University of Illinois Press, 1978), 86–98.

13. Genovese, *Roll, Jordan, Roll*, 542–43.

14. Laurens van der Post, *First Catch Your Eland* (New York: William Morrow, 1978), 21–58; Black, "Food Plants," 24–26ff.; Heiser, *Nightshades, passim*.

15. Hilliard, *Hog Meat and Hoecake*, 61–62; Nevins (ed.), *America Through British Eyes*, 116; Jones (ed.), *The Plantation South*, 222.

16. Savitt, *Medicine and Slavery*, 88; Kenneth Kiple and Virginia Kiple, "Black Tongue and Black Men: Pellagra and Slavery in the Antebellum South," *Journal of Southern History*, XLIII (1977), 411–28.

17. Yetman (ed.), *Life Under the "Peculiar Institution*," 55–56, 257, 270, 337.

Chapter 7

1. Paul W. Gates, *Agriculture and the Civil War* (New York: Alfred A. Knopf, 1965), 6–8, 37, 90, 111–12; Charles P. Roland, *The Confederacy* (Chicago: University of Chicago Press, 1960), 150–51; Francis Butler Simkins and James Welch Patton, *The Women of the Confederacy* (Richmond: Garrett and Massie, 1936), 135.

2. Joe Gray Taylor, "Slavery in Louisiana During the Civil War," *Louisiana History*, VIII (1967), 27–34; Gates, *Agriculture and the Civl War*, 8, 59; Roland, *The Confederacy*, 151; Colonel Charles C. Jones to Mary Jones, May 28, 1863, in Myers (ed.), *Children of Pride*, 1064.

3. Russell, *Diary North and South*, 82–126; Nevins (ed.), *America Through British Eyes*, 285; Katherine M. Jones (ed.), *Heroines of Dixie: Confederate Women Tell Their Story of War* (Indianapolis: Bobbs-Merrill, 1955), 72–73; Myers (ed.), *Children of Pride*, 739.

4. Quoted in Bell Irvin Wiley, *Southern Negroes, 1861–1865* (New Haven: Yale University Press, 1938), 25–6.

5. Simkins and Patton, *Women of the Confederacy*, 142; Gates, *Agriculture and the Civil War*, 24; Mary Jones to Lieutenant Charles C. Jones, Jr., November 5, 1862, the Reverend C. C. Jones to Eliza G. Robarts, December 13, 1862, in Myers (ed.), *Children of Pride*, 984, 989. One of my grandparents was a Confederate veteran who died before my birth. The other three grandparents, however, had all lived through the Civil War and had vivid childhood memories of it.

6. Bell Irvin Wiley, *The Life of Johnny Reb: The Common Soldier of the Confederacy* (Baton Rouge: Louisiana State University Press, 1971), 8.

7. Simkins and Patton, *Women of the Confederacy*, 141; Gates, *Agriculture and the Civil War*, 103.

8. Kate Cumming, *Kate: The Journal of a Confederate Nurse*, ed. Richard Barksdale Harwell (Baton Rouge: Louisiana State University Press, 1959), 248; Simkins and Patton, *Women of the Confederacy*, 140.

9. Simkins and Patton, *Women of the Confederacy*, 128.

10. Gates, *Agriculture and the Civil War*, 37, 59, 112; Roland, *The Confederacy*, 152; Simkins and Patton, *Women of the Confederacy*, 152; Eliza Robarts to the Reverend and Mrs. C. C. Jones, May 20, 1861, Mary S. Mallard to Mary Jones, April 15, 1864, in Myers (ed.), *Children of Pride*, 680, 1160.

11. Quoted in Simkins and Patton, *Women of the Confederacy*, 128.

12. *Ibid.*, 126–28; Gates, *Agriculture and the Civil War*, 38–39.

13. Gates, *Agriculture and the Civil War*, 37, 42–43, 59, 76, 94–95, 112; Cumming, *Kate*, 248; Simkins and Patton, *Women of the Confederacy*, 125; Kane, *Southern Christmas*, 201–203.

14. Wiley, *Southern Negroes*, 24–62; Taylor, "Slavery in Louisiana During the Civil War," 27–34.

15. Wiley, *Life of Johnny Reb*, 90–107.

16. *Ibid.*, 90–107.

17. Gates, *Agriculture and the Civil War*, 111–12, 115; Roland, *The Confederacy*, 150–52; Simkins and Patton, *Women of the Confederacy*, 105, 108; Cumming, *Kate*, 248, 269.

18. Quoted in Roland, *The Confederacy*, 169–70.

19. Vincent H. Cassidy and Amos E. Simpson, *Henry Watkins Allen of Louisiana* (Baton Rouge: Louisiana State University Press, 1964), 105–109; Joseph H. Parks, *Joseph E. Brown of Georgia* (Baton Rouge: Louisiana State University Press, 1977), 236, 257; Wiley, *Life of Johnny Reb*, 40–43; Russell, *Diary North and South*, 170;

Tryon (ed.), *Mirror for Americans*, II, 421; Simkins and Patton, *Women of the Confederacy*, 138–39.

20. Simkins and Patton, *Women of the Confederacy*, 100–107.

Chapter 8

1. Edward C. Hampe, Jr., and Merle Wittenberg, *The Lifeline of America: Development of the Food Industry* (New York: McGraw Hill, 1964), 113–26.

2. Thomas D. Clark, *Pills, Petticoats and Plows: The Southern Country Store* (Norman: University of Oklahoma Press, 1944), 308.

3. Vance, *Human Geography of the South*, 418, 427; Carl Carmer, *Stars Fell on Alabama* (New York: Literary Guild, 1934), 4; Marjorie Kinnan Rawlings, *Cross Creek Cookery* (New York: Charles Scribner's Sons, 1971), 22–24, 209–10; Loughmiller and Loughmiller (eds.), *Big Thicket Legacy*, 39.

4. Richard Osborn Cummings, *The American and His Food: A History of Food Habits in the United States* (Chicago: University of Chicago Press, 1940), 111–18.

5. Vance, *Human Geography of the South*, 418; Clark, *Pills, Petticoats and Plows*, 164; Loughmiller and Loughmiller (eds.), *Big Thicket Legacy*, 39; Marion Cyrenus Blackman, *Look Away! Dixie Land Remembered* (New York: McCall, 1971), 50.

6. Loughmiller and Loughmiller (eds.), *Big Thicket Legacy*, 7, 144; Blackman, *Look Away*, 50; Botkin (ed.), *Treasury of Southern Folklore*, 27, 279–80, 563–64; Carmer, *Stars Fell on Alabama*, 268; Clark, *Pills, Petticoats and Plows*, 155–56, 160, 166; Crabb, *Nashville*, 106, 110–11; Federal Writers Project, *These Are Our Lives: As Told by the People and Written by the Members of the Federal Writers Project of the Works Progress Administration in North Carolina, Tennessee, and Georgia* (Chapel Hill: University of North Carolina Press, 1939), 36, 41, 51, 76; Hilliard, *Hog Meat and Hoecake*, 66–67; Kane, *Southern Christmas*, 38; Morton Rubin, *Plantation Country* (Chapel Hill: University of North Carolina Press, 1962), 24; Vance, *Human Geography of the South*, 426–27, 431.

7. Loughmiller and Loughmiller (eds.), *Big Thicket Legacy*, 143–44; Crabb, *Nashville*, 111; Blackman, *Look Away*, 50; Botkin (ed.), *Treasury of Southern Folklore*, 27; Federal Writers Project, *These Are Our Lives*, 36, 41, 51, 76; Rubin, *Plantation Country*, 24.

8. Botkin (ed.), *Treasury of Southern Folklore*, 27; Nora Miller, *The Girl in the Rural Family* (Chapel Hill: University of North Carolina Press, 1935), 65; Willie Morris (ed.), *The South Today: 100 Years After Appomattox* (New York: Harper & Row, 1965), 102; Rawlings, *Cross Creek Cookery*, 126–29; Daniels, *A Southerner Discovers the South*, 5; Loughmiller and Loughmiller (eds.), *Big Thicket Legacy*, 6, 105; Clark, *Pills, Petticoats and Plows*, 135; Vance, *Human Geography of the South*, 429.

9. Clark, *Pills, Petticoats and Plows*, 44–45, 101, 133, 136–37, 160–61; 166, 168, 170; Botkin (ed.), *Treasury of Southern Folklore*, 279–80, 563–64, 569–70, 572–73, 668; Loughmiller and Loughmiller (eds.), *Big Thicket Legacy*, 143–44; Crabb, *Nashville*, 117; Blackman, *Look Away*, 8, 50, 76; Carmer, *Stars Fell on Alabama*, 268; Hilliard, *Hog Meat and Hoecake*, 66–67; Vance, *Human Geography of the South*, 426–27, 429, 430–31; Margaret Jarman Hagood, *Mothers of the South: Portraiture of the White Tenant Farm Woman* (New York: Arno Press, 1972), 101, 104; Miller, *Girl in the Rural Family*, 17, 77; Huey P. Long, *Every Man a King* (New Orleans: National, 1928), 263–65; Herman Clarence Nixon, *Possum Trot:*

Rural Community, South (Norman: University of Oklahoma Press, 1941), 48;
Kane, *Southern Christmas*, 218; James Agee and Walker Evans, *Let Us Now Praise
Famous Men* (Boston: Houghton Mifflin, 1939), 130–31.
   10. Quoted in Botkin (ed.), *Treasury of Southern Folklore*, 562–63; see also
Vance, *Human Geography of the South*, 425, 428; Blackman, *Look Away*, 48;
Hagood, *Mothers of the South*, 102; Miller, *Girl in the Rural Family*, 46.
   11. Vance, *Human Geography of the South*, 425, 428–29; Hagood, *Mothers of the
South*, 102.
   12. Quoted in Botkin (ed.), *Treasury of Southern Folklore*, 563; Blackman, *Look
Away*, 49; Carmer, *Stars Fell on Alabama*, 66, 93–94, 102.
   13. Vance, *Human Geography of the South*, 425, 429.
   14. Blackman, *Look Away*, 51; quoted in Botkin (ed.), *Treasury of Southern
Folklore*, 564; E. Merton Coulter, *James Monroe Smith, Georgia Planter: Before
Death and After* (Athens: University of Georgia Press, 1961), 174.

Chapter 9

   1. Donald Davidson (ed.), *Selected Essays and Other Writings of John Donald
Wade* (Athens: University of Georgia Press, 1966), 61–70, 104; John T. Trowbridge,
*The Desolate South, 1865–1866: A Picture of the Battle Fields and of the Devas-
tated Confederacy* (Freeport, N.Y.: Books for Libraries Press, 1970), 41; Vance, *Human Geography of the South*, 418; Botkin (ed.), *Treasury of Southern Folklore*, 552;
Crabb, *Nashville*, 101.
   2. Daniels, *A Southerner Discovers the South*, 39, 59. See also Carl Goerch,
Down Home (Raleigh, N.C.: Edwards and Broughton, 1943), 85; A. Neville Barry,
Land of the Light: A Paen of Praise to the Deep South (San Antonio, Tex.: Naylor,
1966), 33; Blackman, *Look Away*, 128–29.
   3. Clark, *Pills, Petticoats and Plows*, 49.
   4. Blackman, *Look Away*, 44–45, 51; Clark, *Pills, Petticoats and Plows*, 167;
Carmer, *Stars Fell on Alabama*, 96; Vance, *Human Geography of the South*, 428–29;
Daniels, *A Southerner Discovers the South*, 160.
   5. Carmer, *Stars Fell on Alabama*, 7; Clark, *Pills, Petticoats and Plows*, 42–43,
228; Harry M. Caudill, *Night Comes to the Cumberlands* (Boston: Little, Brown,
1963), 149; Loughmiller and Loughmiller (eds.), *Big Thicket Legacy*, 87; Botkin
(ed.), *Treasury of Southern Folklore*, 555–56.
   6. Caudill, *Night Comes to the Cumberlands*, 78; Kane, *Southern Christmas*, 121;
Carmer, *Stars Fell on Alabama*, 14. For families who did little or no visting, see
Hagood, *Mothers of the South*, 174–75.
   7. Owsley, *Plain Folk of the Old South*, 98.
   8. *Ibid.*, 110, 105–112; Hagood, *Mothers of the South*, 175–76; Miller, *Girl in the
Rural Family*, 18; Botkin (ed.), *Treasury of Southern Folklore*, 606; William T.
Couch (ed.), *Culture in the South* (Chapel Hill: University of North Carolina Press,
1934), 319–20.
   9. Coulter, *James Monroe Smith*, 180–81.
   10. *Ibid.*, 181–82.
   11. Nixon, *Possum Trot*, 39; Carmer, *Stars Fell on Alabama*, 55; Owsley, *Plain
Folk of the Old South*, 103.
   12. Blackman, *Look Away*, 176; Mody C. Boatright, William M. Hudson, and Allen Maxwell (eds.), *A Good Tale and a Bonny Tune* (Dallas: Southern Methodist
University Press, 1964), 64; Clark, *Pills, Petticoats and Plows*, 56, 74, 268; Crabb,

Nashville, 120–21; Owsley, *Plain Folk of the Old South*, 126–31; Louis B. Wright and H.T. Swedenberg (eds.), *The American Tradition: National Characteristics, Past and Present* (New York: F. S. Crofts, 1941), 193–95.

Chapter 10

1. Lumpkin, *Making of a Southerner*, 158.
2. Paul E. Mertz, *New Deal Policy and Southern Rural Poverty* (Baton Rouge: Louisiana State University Press, 1978), 1–19.
3. *Ibid.*, W. O. Atwater and Charles D. Woods, *Dietary Studies with Reference to the Food of the Negro in Alabama in 1895 and 1896* (Washington, D.C.: Government Printing Office, 1896), 17–19; Miller, *Girl in the Rural Family*, 41; Clark, *Pills, Petticoats and Plows,* 88.
4. Herbert G. Gutman, *The Black Family in Slavery and Freedom, 1750–1925* (New York: Pantheon Books, 1976), 466.
5. Atwater and Woods, *Dietary Studies*, 19–20, 53; Botkin (ed.), *Treasury of Southern Folklore*, 134; Clark, *Pills, Petticoats and Plows*, 156–57; Agee and Evans, *Let Us Now Praise Famous Men*, 115–18; Allison Davis, Burleigh B. Gardner, and Mary R. Gardner, *Deep South: A Social and Anthropological Study of Caste and Class* (Chicago: University of Chicago Press, 1941), 379–81.
6. Clark, *Pills, Petticoats and Plows*, 160; Dorothy Dickens, *A Study of Food Habits of People in Two Contrasting Areas of Mississippi*. Bulletin No. 245, Mississippi Agricultural Experiment Station, Agricultural College (November, 1927), 28.
7. Federal Writers Project, *These Are Our Lives*, 329; Robert Coles, *Migrants, Sharecroppers, Mountaineers* (Boston: Little, Brown, 1971), 599.
8. Federal Writers Project, *These Are Our Lives*, 326, 130, 145–46, 149.
9. Miller, *Girl in the Rural Family*, 55; Rubin, *Plantation Country*, 18; Federal Writers Project, *These Are Our Lives*, 371; George Brown Tindall, *South Carolina Negroes, 1877–1900* (Baton Rouge: Louisiana State University Press, 1966), 288–89; Arthur F. Raper and Ira De A. Reid, *Sharecroppers All* (Chapel Hill: University of North Carolina Press, 1941), 5; Clark, *Pills, Petticoats and Plows*, 44–45; Davis, Gardner, and Gardner, *Deep South*, 386.
10. Cummings, *The American and His Food*, 53–54, 111–18; Davis, Gardner, and Gardner, *Deep South*, 384; Federal Writers Project, *These Are Our Lives*, 229; Hagood, *Mothers of the South*, 129; Emory Q. Hawk, *Economic History of the South* (New York: Prentice Hall, 1934), 525–26; William C. Holley, Ellen Winston, and T. J. Woofter, Jr., *The Plantation South* (Washington, D.C.: Government Printing Office, 1940), 55–56.
11. Caudill, *Night Comes to the Cumberlands*, 184–85; Federal Writers Project, *These Are Our Lives, passim*; George Brown Tindall, *The Emergence of the New South, 1913–1945* (Baton Rouge: Louisiana State University Press, 1967), 477, Vol. X of Wendell Holmes Stephenson and E. Merton Coulter (eds.), *A History of the South*; Mertz, *New Deal Policy and Southern Rural Property*, 1–67.
12. Federal Writers Project, *These Are Our Lives*, 239–40; Harry Ashmore, *An Epitaph for Dixie* (New York: W. W. Norton, 1958), 63; Loughmiller and Loughmiller (eds.), *Big Thicket Legacy*, 191.
13. Robert Coles, *Farewell to the South* (Boston: Little, Brown, 1972), 95; H. Brandt Ayers and Thomas H. Naylor (eds.), *You Can't Eat Magnolias* (New York: McGraw Hill, 1972), 274–75; John Egerton, *The Americanization of Dixie: The Southernization of America* (New York: Harper's Magazine Press, 1974), 107; Jack

E. Weller, *Yesterday's People: Life in Contemporary Appalachia* (Lexington: University Press of Kentucky, 1965), 60; Agricultural Board Division of Biology and Agriculture, National Research Council, *The Quality of Rural Living: Proceedings of a Workshop* (Washington, D.C.: National Academy of Sciences, 1971), 38.

14. Ayers and Naylor (eds.), *You Can't Eat Magnolias*, 275–76, 279–80; Clark, *Pills, Petticoats and Plows*, 264; Cummings, *The American and His Food*, 86; Federal Writers Project, *These Are Our Lives*, 408; Hagood, *Mothers of the South*, 103; Hawk, *Economic History of the South*, 513.

15. C. Vann Woodward, *Origins of the New South, 1877–1913* (Baton Rouge: Louisiana State University Press, 1951), 426–27, Vol. IX of Wendell Holmes Stephenson and E. Merton Coulter (eds.), *A History of the South*.

16. Elizabeth W. Etheridge, *The Butterfly Caste: A Social History of Pellagra in the South* (Westport, Conn.: Greenwood, 1972), *passim*.

17. Ayers and Naylor (eds.), *You Can't Eat Magnolias*, 275–76; Calvin B. Hoover and B. U. Ratchford, *Economic Policies and Resources of the South* (New York: Macmillan, 1951), 30.

18. Coles, *Farewell to the South*, 87–88.

Chapter 11

1. Letitia M. Brewster and Michael F. Jacobson, *The Changing American Diet* (Washington, D.C.: Government Printing Office, 1978), 1–11, *passim*.

2. John Shelton Reed, *The Enduring South: Sub-Culture Persistence in Mass Society* (Lexington, Mass.: Lexington Books, 1972), 84; Thomas D. Clark and Albert D. Kirwan, *The South Since Appomattox: A Century of Regional Change* (New York: Oxford University Press, 1969), 331, 339, 469.

3. Coles, *Farewell to the South*, 90, 101, 173.

4. Morris (ed.), *The South Today*, 113.

5. Egerton, *The Americanization of Dixie*, 106.

Bibliographical Essay

Chapter 1

Especially useful for study of food, drink, and social life on the frontier are William Byrd III's "Secret History of the Dividing Line" and "History of the Dividing Line," both of which are printed in Louis B. Wright (ed.), *The Prose Works of William Byrd of Westover: Narratives of a Colonial Virginian* (Cambridge, Mass: Belknap Press of Harvard University Press, 1966). Also useful are Eugene L. Schwaab (ed.), *Travels in the Old South, Selected from Periodicals of the Time* (Lexington: University Press of Kentucky, 1973), and Francis Harper (ed.), *Travels of William Bartram* (New Haven: Yale University Press, 1958). Superior secondary works include Harriette Arnow's *Seedtime on the Cumberland* (New York: Macmillan, 1960) and *Flowering of the Cumberland* (New York: Macmillan, 1963); Everett Dick, *The Dixie Frontier: A Social History of the Southern Frontier from the First Transmontane Beginnings to the Civil War* (New York: Capricorn Books, 1964); and Thomas D. Clark, *The Rampaging Frontier: Manners and Humor of Pioneer Days in the South and the Middle West* (Indianapolis: Bobbs-Merrill, 1939). Gertrude I. Thomas, *Foods of Our Forefathers* (Philadelphia: F. A. David, 1941); Ray Tannehill, *Food in History* (New York: Stein and Day, 1973); and Ray Allen Billington, *America's Frontier Heritage* (New York: Holt, Rinehart and Winston, 1966) should also be noted.

Chapters 2 and 3

Far too many good books deal with this aspect of antebellum history for all of them to be named here. Good compilations include Harnett T. Kane, *The Southern Christmas Book: The Full Story from the Earliest Times to the Present: People, Customs, Conviviality, Carols, Cooking* (New York: D. McKay, 1958); Benjamin Albert Botkin (ed.), *A Treasury of Southern Folklore: Stories, Ballads, Traditions, and Folkways of the People of the*

South (New York: Crown, 1949); Katherine M. Jones (ed.), *The Planta-tion South* (Indianapolis: Bobbs-Merrill, 1957); Warren S. Tryon (ed.), *A Mirror for Americans: Life and Manners in the United States, 1790–1870, As Recorded by American Travelers* (Chicago: University of Chicago Press, 1952); and Allan Nevins (ed.), *America Through British Eyes* (New York: Oxford University Press, 1948). The letters of the Charles Colcock Jones family, in Robert Manson Myers (ed.), *The Children of Pride: A True Story of Georgia and the Civil War* (New Haven: Yale University Press, 1972), are especially valuable. Joseph G. Baldwin, *The Flush Times of Alabama and Mississippi: A Series of Sketches* (New York: Sagamore Press, 1973), is highly useful, as are Amos Andrew Parker, *A Trip to the West and Texas* (New York: Arno Press, 1973), and Frederick Law Olmsted's *A Jour-ney in the Seaboard Slave States* (New York: Negro Universities Press, 1956) and *Journey in the Back Country* (New York: Shocken Books, 1972).

The most valuable secondary source on antebellum southern food is Sam Bowers Hilliard, *Hog Meat and Hoecake: Food Supply in the Old South* (Carbondale: Southern Illinois University Press, 1972). Its impor-tance can hardly be overestimated. Other important works that greatly aid the researcher are Frank Lawrence Owsley, *Plain Folk of the Old South* (Baton Rouge: Louisiana State University Press, 1949), Arnow's *Flowering of the Cumberland*, Dick's *Dixie Frontier*, and Guion Griffis Johnson, *Ante-Bellum North Carolina: A Social History* (Chapel Hill: University of North Carolina Press, 1937). Two works that emphasize the role of women are Julia Cherry Spruill, *Women's Life and Work in the Southern Colonies* (New York: Russell and Russell, 1969), and Dolores Egger Labbe, "Women in Early Nineteenth-Century Louisiana" (Ph.D. dissertation, University of Delaware, 1975).

Chapter 4

Among the books already mentioned, Jones (ed.), *The Plantation South*; Kane, *Southern Christmas*; Hilliard, *Hog Meat and Hoecake*; and Myers (ed.), *Children of Pride*, tell much about life on large plantations. William Howard Russell, *My Diary North and South*, ed. Fletcher Pratt (New York: Harper and Brothers, 1954), describes the South on the very verge of Civil War. Susan Dabney Smedes, *Memorials of a Southern Planter* (Bal-timore: Cushings and Bailey, 1888); Harriet Martineau, *Society in Amer-ica* (Garden City, N.Y.: Anchor Books, 1962); Katherine Du Pre Lumpkin, *The Making of a Southerner* (New York: Alfred A. Knopf, 1947); and Dix-on Wecter, *The Saga of American Society: A Record of Social Aspiration, 1607–1937* (New York: Charles Scribner's Sons, 1937), are all useful.

Chapter 5

Practically everyone who traveled through the South commented, usually unfavorably, on commercial food and lodging. Among the works already cited, Myers (ed.), *Children of Pride*; Martineau, *Society in America*; Parker, *Trip to the West and Texas*; Olmsted, *Journey in the Seaboard Slave States*; Russell, *Diary North and South*; and Schwaab, (ed.), *Travels in the Old South* are especially useful. Highly interesting, perhaps because their pens were often filled with vitriol, were the Englishman J. S. Buckingham, who wrote *The Slave States of America* (New York: Negro Universities Press, 1968), and that Virginian about to become a Texan, Colonel William F. Gray, whose journal was entitled *From Virginia to Texas, 1835: Diary of Col. William F. Gray, Giving Details of His Journey to Texas and Return in 1835–1836 and Second Journey to Texas in 1837, with Preface by A. C. Gray* (Houston: Fletcher Young, 1965).

Chapter 6

There seems no end to the writing of books on slavery. Fortunately, there is no great disagreement concerning the diet of blacks. Myers (ed.), *Children of Pride*, contains much firsthand information, as does Norman R. Yetman (ed.), *Life Under the "Peculiar Institution": Selections from the Slave Narratives* (New York: Holt, Rinehart and Winston, 1970), and Solomon Northrup, *Twelve Years A Slave*, ed. Sue Eakin and Joseph Logsdon (Baton Rouge: Louisiana State University Press, 1968). Attention should also be called to Eugene Genovese, *Roll, Jordan, Roll: The World the Slaves Made* (New York: Pantheon Books, 1974); Richard C. Wade, *Slavery in the Cities: The South, 1820–1860* (New York: Oxford University Press, 1964); and John Blassingame, *The Slave Community: Plantation Life in the Antebellum South* (New York: Oxford University Press, 1972). The adequacy of slave diet is considered in Todd L. Savitt, *Medicine and Slavery: The Diseases and Care of Blacks in Antebellum Virginia* (Urbana: University of Illinois Press, 1978), and in Kenneth F. Kiple and Virginia H. Kiple, "Black Tongue and Black Men: Pellagra and Slavery in the Antebellum South," *Journal of Southern History*, XLIII (1977), 411–28.

Chapter 7

Russell, *Diary North and South*; Myers (ed.), *Children of Pride*; and Kate Cumming, *Kate: The Journal of a Confederate Nurse*, ed. Richard Barksdale Harwell (Baton Rouge: Louisiana State University Press, 1959), provide firsthand information on southern diet during the Civil War. Essential secondary works are Paul W. Gates, *Agriculture and the Civil War* (New York: Alfred A. Knopf, 1965); Francis Butler Simkins and James Welch Patton, *The Women of the Confederacy* (Richmond: Garrett and Massie, 1936); and Bell Irvin Wiley's *Southern Negroes, 1861–1865* (Baton Rouge: Louisiana State University Press, 1974), and *The Life of Johnny Reb: The Common Soldier of the Confederacy* (Baton Rouge: Louisiana State University Press, 1971).

Chapters 8 and 9

A number of memoirs touch upon the food of the New South. They include Marion Cyrenus Blackman, *Look Away! Dixie Land Remembered* (New York: McCall, 1971); Jonathan Daniels, *A Southerner Discovers the South* (New York: Macmillan, 1938); Carl Carmer, *Stars Fell on Alabama* (New York: Literary Guild, 1934); Herman Clarence Nixon, *Possum Trot: Rural Community, South* (Norman: University of Oklahoma Press, 1941); and Joe Gray Taylor, "The Food of the New South," *Georgia Review,* XX (Spring, 1966), 9–28. A recent oral history project, Campbell Loughmiller and Lynn Loughmiller (eds.), *Big Thicket Legacy* (Austin: University of Texas Press, 1977), describes an area where many characteristics of the eighteenth-century frontier persisted into the twentieth century. Among secondary sources, Thomas D. Clark, *Pills, Petticoats and Plows: The Southern Country Store* (Norman: University of Oklahoma Press, 1944), is invaluable. Other useful books are Margaret Jarman Hagood, *Mothers of the South: Portraiture of the White Tenant Farm Woman* (New York: Arno Press, 1972); Harry M. Caudill, *Night Comes to the Cumberlands* (Boston: Little, Brown, 1963); and Rupert B. Vance, *Human Geography of the South* (Chapel Hill: University of North Carolina Press, 1935).

Chapter 10

The southern poor are revealed in a number of U.S. government studies, including W. O. Atwater and Charles D. Woods, *Dietary Studies with Reference to the Negro in Alabama in 1895 and 1896* (Washington, D.C.: Government Printing Office, 1896); Dorothy Dickens, *A Study of Food Habits of People in Two Contrasting Areas of Mississippi,* Bulletin No. 245, Mississippi Agricultural Experiment Station, Agricultural College (November, 1927); and Federal Writers Project, *These Are Our Lives: As Told by the People and Written by the Members of the Federal Writers Project of the Works Progress Administration in North Carolina, Tennessee, and Georgia* (Chapel Hill: University of North Carolina Press, 1939). Vance's *Human Geography of the South* and Clark's *Pills, Petticoats and Plows* are highly useful. Other good books dealing with the subject are Allison Davis, Burleigh B. Gardner, and Mary R. Gardner, *Deep South: A Social Anthropological Study of Caste and Class* (Chicago: University of Chicago Press, 1941); Paul E. Mertz, *New Deal Policy and Southern Rural Poverty* (Baton Rouge: Louisiana State University Press, 1978); H. Brandt Ayers and Thomas H. Naylor, (eds.), *You Can't Eat Magnolias* (New York: McGraw Hill, 1972); and Elizabeth W. Etheridge, *The Butterfly Caste: A Social History of Pellagra in the South* (Westport, Conn.: Greenwood, 1972). Also, attention should be called to two works by Robert Coles, *Migrants, Sharecroppers, Mountaineers* (Boston: Little, Brown, 1971) and *Farewell to the South* (Boston: Little, Brown, 1972).

Chapter 11

Letitia M. Brewster and Michael F. Jacobson's pamphlet, *The Changing American Diet* (Washington, D. C.: Government Printing Office, 1978), is useful in evaluating modern changes in southern diet, as is John Egerton's *The Americanization of Dixie: The Southernization of America* (New York: Harper's Magazine Press, 1974). This final chapter is based primarily, however, on the author's observations and conclusions derived from living, eating, and drinking in various parts of the South for almost sixty years.

Index

Acadians, 34, 51
Africa: 4, 40, 89; cooking, 88–89
Alabama: 17, 47, 74, 87, 99–100, 121, 128, 131; Mobile, 47, 64, 78, 94, 98, 102; Montgomery, 47, 57, 78, 125; Possum Trot, 134; Wetumka, 78
Alcohol, 43–46, 58–59, 156
Ale, 44, 58
Alligator, 8, 34, 56, 156
Appalachia, 98, 138, 143, 145
Appalachian Mountains, 17, 26, 41, 58, 67, 131
Apples, 41–42, 57–58, 60, 72, 79, 84, 108, 119, 138
Arkansas, 71, 93, 101, 141, 145
Atlantic: Coast, 4, 32, 116; frontier, 12; Ocean, 3, 85; states, 28

Baking: powder, 21, 97, 108, 110; soda, 102, 110
Balls, 46, 51, 61
Bananas, 41, 57
Barbecue, 23, 27, 50, 114, 133–34, 153–54
Batter cake, 122
Beans, 4, 12, 40, 78, 87, 99, 118, 120–21, 126, 133, 141, 145, 154
Bear: 5–6, 8, 10, 32, 115; fat, 5–6; grease, 6–7; hams, 6; hide, 6; meat, 6, 13, 17; sausage, 78; steaks, 6
Beaver tail soup, 8, 17
Beef: 10, 17, 22, 27–28, 47, 55–58, 61, 77, 84–85, 87, 96, 100–101, 103, 113–14, 120, 137, 151–53; Australian, 27; chipped, 28; corned, 27,
108; kidney, 78; pickled, 27; roast, 27, 69, 73, 80, 114, 121, 152, 156; soup bone, 114; steak, 27, 55, 60, 69–70, 78, 114, 120, 122; Stroganoff, 150; tongue, 57–58; tripe, 28, 78
Beer, 12, 44, 46, 59, 129, 153, 156
Berries, 9–10
"Big eating," 18, 53
Biscuits, 21, 30, 54, 56, 58, 70, 72, 94, 100, 108, 110–11, 113, 115, 120, 122, 126–27, 131–34, 137–38, 140, 150, 154
Blackberry: 12, 42, 72, 115, 119; pie, 42; wine, 42, 120
Blacks, 83–91, 94, 100, 104, 111, 118, 132–33, 137, 139–46, 150
Blockade, 95–96, 102
Bobcat, 8–10
Bootleggers, 130
Brandy, 12, 59
Brazil, 4, 40
Bread: 18, 24, 57, 69–71, 77, 80, 84, 91, 98, 135, 146; commercial, 111; "light," 111, 132–33; pudding, 57
Breakfast, 18, 24, 37, 54–55, 70–71, 78, 80–81, 84, 108, 111, 120, 126–27, 140
Brunswick stew, 32, 50, 116, 154
Buffalo, 5, 8
Bullfrogs, 35, 117
Burgoo, 32, 50, 154
Butter, 8, 20, 28–30, 37, 54, 56, 68, 70–71, 76–77, 79, 81, 87, 110–11, 113, 120–22, 127, 152
Buttermilk, 30, 44, 72, 87–88, 110, 121, 135

Cakes, 132–35, 138
Calves: 27, 29, 71, 77, 114; liver, 28
Candy, 43, 134
Canned foods, 108–109, 121, 125–26
Capon, 55–56
Carolinas, 3, 20, 26, 41, 70, 75
Catfish, 9, 34, 86, 116, 127, 153, 156
Cattle, 9–10, 26, 29, 93, 99, 113, 127
Champagne, 49, 55, 57–58
Cheese, 8, 30, 56, 87, 137, 141, 156
Chicken: 31–32, 69, 84, 114–15, 121,
  131, 133; boiled, 30; broiled, 78; and
  dumplings, 31; fried, 30, 72, 111, 114,
  121, 134–35, 152, 153; pie, 31, 132;
  roasted, 30; salad, 114; chickens, 10,
  30–32, 41, 55, 79, 85, 97, 101, 125,
  139, 141, 152–53
Children, 37–38, 42–44, 75, 95, 98,
  102–103, 129, 131, 141, 143–44
Chili, 154
Chocolate, 54, 97
Christmas: 8, 34, 43, 54, 59, 61, 84,
  116, 119; dinner, 81; gifts, 99
Cider, 12, 41–42, 44, 50, 58, 97
Cities, 49, 54, 67, 77–79, 107, 111–12,
  125, 139, 141–42, 149–50, 155
Civil War, 3, 7, 17–18, 21, 24, 26,
  29–30, 32–33, 39–40, 41–42, 44,
  46, 48, 50, 64, 68, 74, 76–78, 84, 88,
  91, 93–104, 107–11, 113–15, 117–19,
  125, 127–32, 134, 144–45, 154–55
Clabber, 20, 29–30, 44, 54
Clergymen, 49, 62
Coca Cola, 129
Cocktail party, 155–57
Coffee: 13, 44, 47, 54, 56–58, 69–72,
  74, 78, 84, 89, 91, 94–96, 113, 120,
  126, 128, 131–33, 140, 156; substitutes, 44, 90, 96–97
Coleslaw, 126, 135
Confederacy: 93–104, 101, 142–43;
  armies, 93–95, 98–99, 101; cavalry,
  101; civilians, 99, 101; commissary,
  100; currency, 77, 103; food riots, 98;
  government, 93; morale, 102; officials, 94, 98; soldiers, 95–96, 100–
  103; women, 98–99, 101–103
Contraband camps, 100
Cookbooks, 19, 150
Cookstoves, 18, 107–109, 140, 151
Corn: 4–5, 7–8, 10, 21, 37, 50, 83,
  94–95, 97, 99, 102, 121, 130; bread,
  6, 8, 13, 20–21, 24, 30, 47, 56–58,
  69–72, 78–79, 83–84, 88, 91, 95,
  99–104, 108–11, 118, 120–22,
  126–27, 134, 137, 140, 154; cake, 56;
  cribs, 94, 101; fields, 39–40, 116;
  fritters, 37; green, 37, 87, 89, 118;
  meal, 11, 21, 37, 83–84, 102, 104,
  109–10, 112, 133, 137, 139–40,
  144–45, 150, 154; meal mush, 37;
  pones, 20, 84, 91, 110, 121, 133;
  roasting ears, 11, 37, 84; shuckings,
  46, 50, 132; whiskey, 12, 44–45, 130,
  141
Cottage cheese, 30
Cowpeas, 4, 12, 22, 24, 39, 41, 87–88,
  90–91, 94, 99, 101–102, 118,
  120–21, 126, 141, 152, 154
Cows: 9, 27–28, 30, 41, 44, 85, 87, 97,
  117, 125, 139, 141, 145; milch, 28, 97,
  101, 117, 152
Crab, 33–34, 56, 117, 156
Cracklins, 24, 112, 133
Crayfish, 34, 117, 154, 156
Cream, 29, 42, 54, 58, 119
Creoles, 20, 34, 46, 51, 79–80
Crop lien, 137, 139
Custard, 56, 133, 153

Dancing, 46, 48, 50–51, 60
Deer, 6–7, 154
Desserts, 43, 47, 57, 77, 120–21
Diet, 32, 42–43, 53, 104, 107–109, 112,
  115, 125, 139, 141–42, 144, 150, 152
Dinner: 18, 55–56, 73, 84, 120–21,
  126, 131, 140; party, 32, 62
Dishes: 20, 73, 79–80, 109, 116, 134,
  149–50, 154; china, 19, 53, 121;
  earthenware, 19; European, 53;
  pewter, 19, 53; wooden, 19
District of Columbia, 77
Dove, 33, 56, 115, 152
Drink, 12–13, 49–50, 68
Drunkenness, 13, 45, 58
Ducks, 31, 33, 55–56, 78, 85, 114–15,
  121, 152
Dumplings, 32, 116, 121, 133

East Coast, 39, 68
Eggnog, 59
Eggs, 10, 20, 24, 31–32, 54–56,

69–70, 72, 78, 85, 102, 110, 113–14, 120–21, 125, 135, 138, 154
England: 19, 23–24, 30, 41, 89, 95; Englishmen, 18, 68, 79, 80
Europe, 8, 20, 53

Farms, 31, 48, 58, 83–84, 87, 94, 107, 121, 125–26, 128, 140, 142
Farmers, 18, 25, 31, 37–38, 41, 46–47, 50, 55, 59, 83, 89, 94–95, 108, 112–13, 118–21, 125, 137–41, 151
Fast foods, 152–53
Fireplaces, 18–19, 27, 38, 84, 89, 107, 140
Fish, 4, 8, 17, 33–34, 47, 54, 57, 69, 78, 81, 83–86, 94, 99, 108, 110, 114, 116–17, 126, 141, 151–53
Flies, 71, 79, 117–18
Florida, 9, 26–27, 35, 41, 63, 96–97, 117, 119, 120, 151, 154
Fowl, 56, 73
Frontier, 3–14, 17, 47, 71, 83, 89, 115, 154
Frontiersmen, 5–12, 46
Fruit, 22, 42, 47, 57, 87–88, 94, 104, 108–109, 118–21, 151
Funerals, 46, 49, 134

General store, 107, 112, 129, 133, 137, 139, 141
Georgia: 26, 28, 35, 41, 45, 57, 60, 70–71, 74, 101–102, 117, 122, 133, 154; Athens, 47, 77; Atlanta, 127, 131; Augusta, 70; Columbus, 22, 70, 77; Macon, 47, 70, 79; Milledgeville, 70; Savannah, 47, 54, 76, 81, 126
Goose, 31, 33, 55, 79, 85, 114–15, 121, 152
Grain, 12, 22, 130
Grapes, 9, 42, 56, 119
Gravy, 68, 70, 73, 111, 115, 120, 140, 146
Grease, 26, 110–11, 118, 144
Great Depression, 142–43
Great Valley, 4, 41
Greens, 24, 55, 77, 91, 120–21, 127, 143, 151
Grits, 11, 37, 54, 71, 87, 118, 120, 146, 154
Grocery store, 108, 111–13, 116, 126
Guinea fowl, 31, 56, 114, 121

Gulf of Mexico: 41; coast, 32, 42, 116
Gumbo, 20, 33–34, 51, 57, 154

Hens, 30–32
Hoecake, 83–84, 89, 110
Hogs: 5, 22–24, 26, 30, 38, 85, 95, 99, 101, 111–13, 125, 127, 133, 137, 152; killing, 23–25, 84, 91, 112–13, 125, 140; razorback, 10, 23, 93; wild, 8, 10
Hog's head cheese, 24
Hominy, 11, 37, 55, 57, 72, 78, 87, 126
Honey, 42, 96–97, 126–27
Hospitality, 13, 46–47, 49, 59–60, 64, 68, 103, 130, 132, 156
Hotels, 51, 71, 73–80, 126, 129, 156
House raising, 46, 49, 50, 132
Hushpuppies, 110, 116, 127

Ice, 34, 128, 152
Ice cream, 30, 55, 57–58, 126, 153
Indians: 3–5, 13, 26, 41, 47, 89, 108, 118; example, 12; Territory, 27
Infare, 48–49
Inns, 70–71, 75, 77
Ireland, 5, 43
Irish, 5, 68
Irish potatoes, 4, 39–40, 57, 76, 80, 118, 120, 126, 133, 135, 143

Jars, 42, 109

Kentucky: 5–6, 25, 32, 63, 71, 74, 154; Louisville, 8, 34, 72–73
Kerosene: 108, 140, 152; lamp, 108; stove, 108
Kettles, 18–19
Kitchen, 18–19, 107–108, 151

Ladles, 12, 19
Lamb, 10, 28, 114, 151
Lard, 6, 22, 24, 26, 37, 40, 102, 109–10, 139–40
Lemon: 128; lemonade, 41, 97, 134
Liqueurs, 59, 102
Log cabin, 18, 54
Logrolling, 46, 49–50, 132
Louisiana: 7, 20, 26–27, 31, 33–35, 37, 40–41, 44, 46–48, 54, 62, 80, 86, 87, 93, 96, 101–102, 114, 117, 120–21, 128–29, 141, 143, 154; Avery Island, 95; Baton Rouge, 126;

Fort Jessup, 72; Lake Providence, 71; Mandeville, 74; Monroe, 32, 71; Natchitoches, 71, 79; New Orleans, 41, 47, 51, 59, 67–68, 71, 73–75, 79, 91, 96, 126, 129, 150, 156; Port Hudson, 93
Louisianians, 45, 74, 156

Mardi Gras, 51, 156
Maryland: 3, 61, 72, 117; Baltimore, 63, 76, 78, 126
Meat, 19, 21–22, 24–25, 43, 48, 57–58, 69–71, 77, 80, 84–86, 88–89, 91, 93, 95, 99–101, 103, 109, 111–14, 120–21, 125–26, 131, 137, 140, 143, 151
Melons, 29, 42, 96, 119, 121, 133, 154
Milk, 8–9, 12, 20, 22, 28–29, 37, 39, 44, 47, 54, 56–57, 70–72, 76–77, 81–88, 91, 97, 101, 110, 120–22, 126, 132, 135, 140–41, 146, 152
Ministers: Baptist, 50; Methodist, 50, 70; Protestant, 46
Mint julep, 45, 59, 63
Mississippi: 17, 20, 38, 50, 58, 70, 95, 140, 145; Holly Springs, 68–69; Natchez, 72, 78; Ocean Springs, 74; Raymond, 63; Vicksburg, 79, 93; Woodville, 62
Mississippi Delta, 143, 145
Mississippi River, 5–6, 9, 14, 32, 39, 90, 93, 96
Missouri, 63, 101
Molasses, 43, 70, 84, 88, 91, 96, 111, 113, 120, 122, 138–40, 150
Mortar and pestle, 11, 19
Muscadines, 9, 42
Music, 50–51
Mutton, 10, 22, 28, 55–56, 58, 69, 76–77, 85, 87, 114

Negro. *See* Blacks
New Deal, 107, 138–39, 142, 145
New England, 12, 44, 67
New South, 109, 113–15, 117–18, 120, 132, 139, 141
North, 23, 39, 72, 74, 78–79, 93, 96, 119, 125, 132, 139
North Carolina: 21, 45, 54, 58, 61, 75, 99, 126, 132, 145, 154; Bladensboro, 98; Salisbury, 98; Tarboro, 70; Wilmington, 102

Northerners, 21, 50, 79–80
Nuts, 9, 42, 58, 60, 119, 156

Old Southwest, 4, 14
Opossum, 6, 8, 10, 32, 42, 56, 86, 99, 116, 154
Oranges, 41, 57, 84
Orchards, 87, 119, 125
Oven, 21, 38, 108
Oyster: 33–34, 56–57, 61, 73, 78, 94, 116–17, 126, 141, 150, 156; bars, 68; patties, 60; pie, 79; saloons, 94; sauce, 56; soup, 77

Panther, 8, 10, 17
Passenger pigeon, 8, 33, 78
Peach: 41–42, 56, 108; brandy, 12, 41, 45, 50
Peanut, 4, 40
Pellagra, 91, 138, 143–46
Pepper, 4, 40, 58, 89, 97, 112–13, 118
Persimmon: 9, 42; beer, 12, 50, 97
Pickles, 57–58, 126, 133–34, 156
Picnic, 133–34
Piedmont, 3–4, 20, 26, 41, 138, 141–42
Pie, 56–58, 77, 119, 127, 131, 133, 135
Pig. *See* Hog; Pork
Pioneers, 3, 5, 8–10, 12, 17, 37, 89
Plantation: 18–20, 23, 26, 31, 33, 41, 48, 54–57, 60–61, 83, 87–88, 90, 94, 98–100, 119, 142, 156; commissary, 112, 137, 139
Planter, 18, 20, 25, 28–29, 38, 46–47, 53–54, 56, 58–62, 84–85, 89, 93–95, 103, 119, 130
Plums, 9, 42, 119
Poor white, 137–45
Pork: 6, 10, 17, 21–22, 32, 39, 47, 55–58, 61, 73, 81, 87, 93, 95–97, 104, 115, 139–40, 153; backbone, 24, 26, 91, 112, 126, 133; bacon, 20, 22, 24–26, 54, 69–70, 72, 77–78, 96, 99–100, 102, 111–12, 120, 137; boiled, 22, 84; brains, 25, 112; chitterlings, 24, 26, 91, 112; chops, 26, 95–96, 114, 121; cured, 25, 28, 57, 85, 95, 99–100, 126; ears, 24, 112; eating, 22, 112; fat, 27, 69, 112; fatback, 25, 84, 112, 137, 138, 141, 150; feet, 24, 70, 78, 112; fresh, 25, 57, 84, 95, 112, 132; fried, 54, 70–71; ham, 25–26, 54–58, 61, 69, 77, 81,

84, 90, 94, 111–13, 120–22, 126,
131–33, 135, 137, 151, 153–54, 156;
ham hock, 37, 39; jowls, 26, 37, 77,
91, 112; kidneys, 24; liver, 24, 26,
112, 121; loin, 112; pickled, 25, 96;
ribs, 54, 121, 125; roast, 58, 131; salt,
47, 69, 89, 118, 144; sausage, 24–26,
54, 112–13, 126, 137; shoulders,
25–26, 112, 137; skins, 153; snouts,
112; tail, 24, 112; tenderloin, 24;
tongue, 24
Pot liquor, 91, 118
Potato house, 38, 118
Pots, 18–19, 89, 109, 112, 118, 140
Poultry, 10, 24, 31, 69, 76, 97, 114, 151
Predators, 10, 28, 31
Preserves, 42, 58, 111, 119–20, 122,
126, 132, 134
Prohibition, 129–30, 155
Protein, 83, 137–38
Pudding, 73, 77, 121, 154
Pumpkins, 4, 12, 40, 58
Punch, 59, 155

Quail, 8, 33, 54, 56, 81, 115–17, 132,
154

Rabbit, 8, 32, 77, 84, 86, 99, 116, 154
Raccoon, 6, 8, 10, 32, 86, 99, 116, 154
Railroads, 34, 39, 107
Rebel. *See* Confederate
Recipes, 19–20
Red-eye gravy, 26, 111, 113, 120
Red River Valley, 101
Refrigeration, 29, 128
Refrigerator, 128, 152
Refugees, 101, 103
Resorts, 67, 74–79
Restaurants, 67–68, 111, 114, 126
Rice, 7, 26, 34, 40, 54, 57, 60, 78, 84,
87, 102, 133, 141, 154
Robins, 8, 33, 78, 115
Rum, 12, 44, 51, 55, 70, 156
Rye bread, 4, 20

Salt, 25, 70, 95–96, 99, 110, 112
Scotch-Irish, 4–5, 12–13, 39, 44
Seafood, 20, 33–34, 57, 73, 120
Servants, 61–63, 70, 75–78, 81, 141
Settlers, 5, 9–10, 12, 25
Sharecroppers, 91, 104, 111, 119, 138,
140, 142, 151

Sheep, 10, 28, 58, 85
Shellfish, 4, 33
Shenandoah Valley, 68, 74–75,
100–101, 119
Shirley Plantation, 55, 58
Shortening, 6, 24, 58, 110, 112, 133
Shrimp, 33, 55–56, 73, 117, 150, 152,
156
Silverware, 19, 53
Slaves: 20, 27–28, 30, 33, 38, 41, 44,
50, 53, 59, 61, 64, 68, 72, 81, 96, 104,
119, 151; diet, 83–91, 99–100
Smokehouse, 25, 85, 90, 94, 101, 121,
132, 150
Soft drinks, 50, 129, 135, 141, 153
Soldiers, 28, 94–95, 98
Sorghum, 43, 88, 96, 111, 122
Soup, 8, 32, 34, 55–57, 121, 126,
154
Souse. *See* Hog's head cheese
South Carolina: 6, 13, 20, 35, 63, 75,
87, 101, 117, 120–21, 137, 145, 154;
Beaufort, 56, 58; Caesar's Head, 126;
Charleston, 41, 47, 51, 54, 56, 60, 67,
76, 78, 102, 126, 150; Georgetown,
70; Greenville, 143; Orangeburg, 70;
Pendleton, 72
South Carolinians, 76, 103
Soybeans, 39, 141
Spaniards, 26, 141
Spit, 19, 28, 89
Springhouse, 29–30
Squab, 31, 114
Squirrel, 8, 32, 115
Steamboat, 34, 72–74
Steer, 27, 58
Stew, 7, 32–34, 133
Stewpot, 8, 12, 89
Strawberries, 58, 77, 156
Suckling pig, 23, 56, 81
Sugar, 42–43, 45, 58, 71, 81, 96,
108–10, 119, 127, 130
Supper, 18, 30, 37, 58, 69–72, 108, 111,
121–22, 126, 134–35, 140
Sweet potato: 4, 11, 17, 32, 37–41,
55–57, 72, 84, 86–87, 89–91, 94,
99, 101, 116, 118, 126, 133, 140;
baked, 50; beds, 38; coffee, 38, 44;
home brew, 38, 97; pie, 38, 121;
seed, 37; slips, 38; varieties, 38;
vines, 22, 38
Swine. *See* Hogs

Tablecloth, 53, 55, 71, 121
Tavern, 45, 50, 68–71, 73–74, 77
Tea, 13, 44, 57–58, 78, 97, 121, 126–27, 135
Temperance, 46, 130
Tenants, 138–39, 144
Tennessee: 25, 70, 74, 94–95, 113; Blountville, 47; Franklin, 100; Jonesboro, 47; Memphis, 34, 77, 80, 125, 140; Nashville, 45, 54, 57, 80–81, 100, 113, 120
Terrapin soup, 35, 55, 117
Texas, 9, 17, 26–27, 40–41, 63, 71–72, 84, 93, 115, 119, 134, 143, 154
Tidewater, 4, 54, 84
Toast, 78, 111
Tobacco chewing, 74, 78, 80
Toddy, 13, 59, 63
Tomatoes, 4, 40, 117, 126
Town, 28, 32, 41, 49, 51, 54, 58, 77, 83, 85, 90, 97–99, 103, 107, 111–12, 117, 125–28, 130, 141–42, 155
Townsmen, 18, 41, 47, 59, 97, 119, 125, 140
Travelers, 18, 20–22, 38, 43–45, 47, 60, 67, 69, 72–73, 77–78, 86, 126, 137
Turkey, 7–8, 17, 31, 33, 38, 55–57, 60, 72, 79, 81, 85, 114–15, 121, 126, 131
Turnips: 41, 77, 118; greens, 11, 37, 47, 72, 87, 91, 121, 126, 133, 154
Turtle: 8, 31, 34–35, 56–57; sauce piquant, 117, 154; soup, 56, 73, 117

Veal, 8, 27, 69
Vegetable: 5, 11–12, 17, 26, 32, 37, 47–48, 57, 61, 69, 73, 77, 87–89, 91, 94, 101, 104, 117–18, 120–21, 151–52; garden, 12, 40–41, 84, 97, 109, 125, 139, 141, 145, 151, 153
Venison, 6–8, 17, 20, 32, 56–57, 72,

77, 85, 115, 154, 156
Vinegar, 27, 42, 58, 97, 114
Virginia: 4, 34, 40, 51, 55–56, 60–61, 63, 69–70, 76–77, 95, 113, 117, 154; Abingdon, 69; Appomattox, 17; Fairfield, 69; Jamestown, 3, 30, 55; Old Point Comfort, 69; Petersburg, 99–100; Richmond, 98, 101; Wythe Court House, 69
Virginians, 10, 50, 55, 58, 61, 68–69, 71
Vitamins, 37–38, 138, 144–46

Waffles, 54, 58
Washington, D.C., 53, 61, 78
Water, 12, 19, 43, 45, 47, 83, 89, 102, 109, 111, 114, 120, 127, 130, 155
Waterfowl, 8, 20, 32, 73, 115, 154
Watering places, 74
Weddings, 46, 48–49, 61–62, 134, 139
Wells, 12, 90, 102, 127
West Indies, 12, 44, 50, 58
West Virginia, 69
Wheat: 11, 70; bread, 4, 20–21, 54, 69, 83; flour, 21, 91, 108, 110, 133, 137, 139–40
Whiskey, 12–13, 34, 43–45, 47, 49–50, 56, 70, 79–80, 90, 102, 129–30, 132, 134, 146, 155–56
Willard's Hotel, 78
Wine, 12, 44, 46, 54–55, 57–60, 63, 68, 73, 78–80, 94, 102, 119, 129, 131–32, 146, 156
Wolves, 5, 10
Wool, 10, 28
Work frolics, 46, 49–50
World War II, 27, 37, 91, 104, 109–10, 113, 116, 120, 138–39, 142, 145, 155

Yeast, 12, 21, 130